Beyond Biblical Criticism

D1490332

To Lilian
    with love
    from Arthur.

BEYOND BIBLICAL CRITICISM

Encountering Jesus in Scripture

ARTHUR WAINWRIGHT

LONDON
SPCK

First published in Great Britain in 1982 by SPCK
  Holy Trinity Church
  Marylebone Road
  London NW1 4DU
and in the USA by John Knox Press

Printed in the USA
ISBN 0 281 03786 8

To my wife
Betty

Preface

When the Scriptures are studied according to the principles of biblical criticism, a great deal of emphasis is laid on the need to avoid being controlled by the presuppositions of faith. The Bible, it is argued, must be treated with the same objectivity as any other book. While this approach is necessary and valuable, it is also important to study the Bible from the viewpoint of faith. The intention of this volume is to present a method of biblical interpretation which is unquestionably Christian. When Jesus is allowed to be the interpreter of the Scriptures, a truly Christian interpretation of them takes place. Such an interpretation takes account of the work of biblical criticism, but at the same time recognizes the need to understand the relevance of the Bible for the present day in the light of the Christian faith. Whatever other influences may play a part in the study of the Bible, Jesus himself is the guiding and controlling influence behind a Christian interpretation of it.

I should like to express my gratitude to June Caldwell for help with the typing, and to my wife for assistance and encouragement at many stages in the preparation of this work.

Contents

1 The Need for a Christian Interpretation of the Bible 1

2 Two Approaches to Jesus: Criticism and Faith 11

3 The Biblical Jesus: The Gospels and the Acts 21

4 The Biblical Jesus: The Epistles and the Book of
  Revelation 35

5 The New Testament in the Light of Jesus 47

6 The Old Testament in the Light of Jesus 57

7 Letting the New Testament Speak for Today 67

8 Discovering Jesus in the Old Testament 81

9 Letting the Old Testament Speak for Today 91

10 Where People Go Wrong 101

11 Smorgasbord Theology 111

12 Finding the Way 119

Notes 131

Index 151

1
The Need for a Christian Interpretation of the Bible

Many readers of the Bible are like sailors cast adrift on the ocean with a vast load of provisions and clothing, but no map or compass. They are uncertain of the meaning of the Scripture and unsure of its relevance for daily life. They wander backwards and forwards through its pages, often perplexed by its contents. Large areas of it appear to have little significance for them. As they venture into the study of the Bible, they lack any guiding principle, which can give them a sense of direction.

This plight is shared by preachers and teachers as well as by those who look to them for instruction. It is the custom to initiate prospective ministers and Bible teachers into the mysteries of biblical criticism. They are trained in the techniques which scholars have used to investigate the Scriptures. They are encouraged to take apart the sacred writings, as though they were amputating the limbs of a body. Unfortunately, when they set themselves to the task of making the Scriptures relevant for today, many of them are unable to put the pieces together again. They have nothing to work with but a collection of dismembered limbs. They have no sense of a living and integrated body of Scripture.

In this situation there is a strong temptation for preachers to resort to exhortations, from which the main themes of the Christian gospel have been silently excluded. Where there is no confidence that the Bible has a relevant and clear message, there is no eagerness to expound it. Scripture becomes a medium for the communication of views which are held independently of it. Preachers who find their chief inspiration in psychology or philosophy or even in national pride, quote the Bible in support of their opinions, but the biblical allusions are an attractive decoration to draw people to the edifice of the preacher's thought. They are not the stones on which it is built.

If the plight of many of the recipients of a theological education is to lack any clear principle for the use and interpretation of Scripture, the plight of those who seek their guidance is no better. A large number of people, both inside and outside the Church, are ignorant of the Bible. They are acquainted with very little of its contents. Their knowledge of its most famous stories and best known teaching is either non-existent or shaky. The Bible is one of the world's greatest victims of lip-service. Its praises are sounded throughout Christendom. It is exalted as the Word of God, the guide to life, and the most precious of all books, but it is rarely read. The presence of a copy of the Bible on a bookshelf is no guarantee that its pages have been opened.

When people who have neglected the Bible begin to read it, perplexity overwhelms them. They have been given a misleading impression of the nature of its contents. Having heard the rapturous tributes which have been paid to it, they imagine it to contain a lucid and orderly statement of Christian doctrines together with a comprehensive set of rules for the conduct of daily life. They assume that these doctrines and rules will be expressed in language which can be clearly understood by anyone of average intelligence. When they actually begin to read the Bible, however, their illusions are soon dispelled. Some of the familiar stories, sayings and parables cause them no serious trouble. But other passages bewilder them. They cannot follow the thread of the argument in the prophets or Paul's letters. The train of thought in the Psalms is frequently obscure to them, and the symbolism of Daniel and the Book of Revelation is difficult to interpret. To add to their disappointment, the Bible contains no systematic account of Christian doctrine and no comprehensive guide to Christian conduct.

History or Literature or Scripture?

One of the reasons for the widespread ignorance and neglect of the Bible is the failure to study it sufficiently from the viewpoint of faith. All too often it is assumed that a serious examination of the Scriptures can only treat them as historical documents. In a great deal of modern investigation the Bible is regarded as a collection of materials for research into ancient history and culture. Scholars claim to approach it without any presuppositions of faith. If they have any personal religious beliefs about it, they put them in cold storage whenever they indulge in scholarship. The books of the Old and New Testaments, they maintain, are to be treated in the same way as any other documents used for research into the history, religion and culture of the ancient world. Viewed in this light, Old Testament scholarship is part of the study of the ancient Near East, and New Testament scholarship is part of the study of Graeco-Roman civilization.

Some modern critics put their emphasis on the Bible as literature. They vary in their interests in this field of investigation. Some of them concentrate on an inquiry into the authorship and sources of the biblical books, and the purposes and situations for which they were written. Others concentrate on an analysis of the form and structure of the books and the passages contained in them. Yet others combine both these aspects of literary criticism. But whichever kind of inquiry they undertake, they claim to be objective and to examine the Bible without any assumptions of religious belief.

The study of the Bible as historical material and as literature is a worthy enterprise, not to be despised, but it is not purely historical and literary concerns which have led people to become students of the biblical writings. A large number, at any rate of those who undertake the study of their own free choice, are attracted to the Bible because they regard it as Scripture. They read it not because of a detached interest in Scripture as a particular kind of literature, but because they regard the Old and New Testaments as sacred writings which are vehicles of a unique divine revelation. Ironically, the concern which has led many people to become students of the Bible is not uppermost in the minds of some of its teachers. A large proportion of the students regard it primarily as Scripture. Many of the teachers treat it primarily as literature or historical source-material. It is indeed legitimate for a teacher to point out that there are more dimensions to the study of a subject than the pupils imagine; but it is legitimate also to consider if the reasons for a student's interest in the subject are valid ones. Sometimes the impression is given that the study of the Bible in the light of faith is an inferior activity to academic research. When this impression is given, the kind of inquiry, which is needed for the Bible to be used as Scripture, is often stifled.

It is as Scripture, however, that most people regard the Bible when they are attracted to the study of it. Many are the theories about its inspiration and authority, but whatever theory is adopted, the Bible is prominent in the Church because it is assumed to have a unique function in relation to the Christian faith. Within the Church it is the text for preaching and teaching, because it is believed to provide access to divine truth, and, above all, to Jesus Christ himself. It is a collection of documents of faith, and deserves to be read from the viewpoint of faith. It is not sufficient for it to be treated as a collection of historical source-material or an anthology of works of literature. It needs to be studied as Scripture.

There have always been scholars, who have given recognition to this aspect of biblical study. The great commentators of the past had no hesitation in approaching the books of the Bible in this way, but in recent years, this approach has been often neglected. Fortunately, interest in it continues, and recognition is being given to the need to understand the Bible as Scripture. When the Bible is regarded in this light, attention begins to be paid to the interpretations given by writers in past generations. Instead of concentrating mainly on what modern scholars have said about it, the interpreter examines the impact which it has made on people, both Jewish and Christian, who have accepted it as their Scripture.

Even this kind of investigation could become merely historical, and confine itself to an examination of other people's reaction to the books of the Bible. People who read the Bible from the viewpoint of faith are people who can say, 'This is my Scripture'.[1] They do not sit on the fence theologically, holding themselves aloof from any commitment of faith. They are ready to descend into the arena, where men and women live by belief in the divine revelation to which the Bible bears witness. There is a time for sitting on the fence. There is also a time for coming down into the arena; a time for reading Scripture in the light of faith; a time for letting it function in daily life.

A Christian Interpretation

The Bible needs a method of interpretation which is intelligible, honest, and unquestionably Christian. As the Church's Scripture, it needs to be understood and used by Christian people. It is not satisfactory for it to merely be in their possession, nor is it satisfactory for it to be read without understanding. A Bible which is read but not understood is of no more use than a Bible left unopened on a bookshelf. It is like a sealed tomb, concealing treasures that never see the light of day.

If it is to function as Christian Scripture, a method of interpretation must be found which is distinctively and unmistakably Christian; it is not sufficient to look at it merely from the position of modern scholarship. A critical inquiry into the books of the Bible will provide important information about the ideas contained in them. It will give evidence about the circumstances in which they were written, the sources which they used, their literary form and structure, the trustworthiness of their manuscript, and the meaning of various words and phrases. It will raise questions about the authorship of the books, their date and their historical reliability. It will discuss their relationship to the culture within which they were written. Such information can be of great assistance in making the Bible intelligible to the modern world, but it does not of itself produce Christian interpretation.

It is also unsatisfactory to assume that, if we try to read the Bible without doctrinal presuppositions, it will 'speak to us' or 'interpret us'. Whether we admit it or not, we set limits to what we allow the Bible to say to us. People who claim to let it 'speak to them' or 'interpret them', usually dictate the terms on which they allow it to influence them. They have open or hidden points of resistance to its message. Some people refuse to let it say anything to them about sexual morality. Others do not let it speak to them about violence or dishonesty. Others will not allow it to tell them about a future life. Before the Bible can adequately 'speak to us' or 'interpret us', we need a standard by which we can interpret it, a standard which is openly recognized and which is clearly Christian.

Moreover, the books of the Bible do not always speak with a united voice. The teaching of Jeremiah is not the same as that of the Book of Exodus. The message of Paul does not have the same emphases as that of the Book of Revelation. To crown it all, the New Testament explicitly sets limits to the authority of the Old. Under these circumstances, if we just let the Bible speak to us, it will give conflicting interpretations of God's will for us. A key is needed to unlock the Scriptures, in order that Jesus Christ himself may speak to us through them. Otherwise we shall be in danger of letting the Bible tell us only what we want to hear.

The most obviously Christian standard for the interpretation of the Bible is Jesus Christ. If the word 'Christian' is not clearly related to him, its usage becomes thoroughly deceptive. He is the essential key to its meaning. Without him the word loses its identity, and becomes a cipher which may be used to designate a bewildering selection of ideas and aspirations. The wide variety of senses in which the word is used causes frequent confusion. Many people who have made no profession of Christian faith and have maintained no association with the organized Church would be deeply insulted by the insinuation that they were not real Christians. The word 'Christian' is synonymous for them with 'upright' or 'good-living'. They pride themselves on bearing the name of Christ, even though they have no understanding of the Christian message, no interest in the Church, and no desire to learn about Jesus. 'Christ' is also frequently used as a description of an admired adherent of another religion. 'Good-living' Jews or Moslems or Hindus may be given the compliment of being described as better Christians than many people who attend church. Even though they may have explicitly rejected Christianity, these adherents of other religions are described as Christian because there is a Christ-like element in their conduct. Such uses of the word, however, are misleading. The term 'Christian' is deceptive unless it refers to a person who accepts Jesus of Nazareth as the Christ, or unless, in the case of a child, it refers to someone who belongs to the community of the Church.

It is not an arbitrary decision to limit the word 'Christian' to an outlook on life which is focused on Jesus in this way. The normal usage of the word 'Christ' is with reference to Jesus of Nazareth as the fulfilment of the Jewish expectation of a Messiah. Both 'Christ' and 'Messiah' mean 'Anointed One', the former being derived from the Greek and the latter from the Hebrew and the Aramaic. The usage of the word 'Christ' has been perpetuated because Jesus has been regarded as the Messiah, but that usage has often been distorted. When people talk of the living Christ or the true Christ in men and women, they may well be referring to their own particular ideal of humanity or to some mystical experience quite independent of Jesus of Nazareth, but because the word normally refers to Jesus, they can be seriously misunderstood. The use of the words 'Christian' and 'Christ' has been perpetuated because people believe that Jesus is the saviour of men and women and the revealer of God. To use the words in relation to other aspirations and ideals is thoroughly misleading.

A Christian is someone who accepts Jesus as the Christ; and Christian interpretation accepts Jesus as the interpreter. One of the distinctive features of Christianity is Jesus's function of interpretation. In the Sermon on the Mount he interprets the Jewish Law in a highly radical fashion[2] and in the closing episodes of Luke's Gospel he interprets all that the Scriptures say about himself.[3] In his earthly life and during his resurrection appearances he expounded only Jewish Scriptures. Since there were at that time no specifically Christian writings, it could not have been otherwise. Yet it is not just the Old Testament which needs Jesus as the interpreter. The New Testament needs him also. His presence within its pages makes it Christian, and he is the clue to its meaning.

Honesty and Intelligibility

Two requirements are necessary if Jesus is to be the interpreter. The first of them is *honesty*. Any interpretation, in which he has a part, refuses to falsify the meaning of the Scriptures. Questions raised by critical scholarship are taken seriously. It is recognized that scholars have doubted whether Moses wrote the books of the Law or Paul wrote all the letters ascribed to him. It is accepted that doubts have been raised about the accuracy of the records of Jesus's life and teaching. An honest inquirer must admit the existence of these questions.

Honesty also forbids that viewpoints should be advocated in the name of Jesus, when they contradict the essential elements of his teaching. There is a persistent tendency for the support of Jesus to be claimed for views far removed from his. He is depicted as a militant patriot, or a man of loose morals—anything that suits the prevailing mood of the times. Honest inquirers resist the temptation to force Jesus into the mould of their preconceived ideas. An impartial examination of the Scriptures will avoid misleading arguments which twist the original meaning of the writers to suit modern presuppositions. It will not employ the Bible to support views, which are far removed from the intention of the writers.

Another requirement for Christian interpretation is *intelligibility*. The books of the Bible were not written for the exclusive use of an intellectual elite. They were intended for ordinary people to read or, if they could not read, to hear. Even when, like the Book of Revelation, they contain hidden meanings, the unravelling of them does not require great intelligence, but the possession of the key to their meaning. As Paul says, in the early Church 'not many were wise', as the world judges wisdom.[4] The first Christians were distinguished neither by the refinement of their education nor by the acuteness of their intellects. There were some great intellects among them, like Paul himself, but brain power was not the endowment most highly valued by them, and the biblical writers do not assume that their readers were intellectually brilliant. Their writings were intended to be understood by ordinary people. Even when a book of the Bible is directly addressed to one person, as are the letters to Philemon, Timothy and Titus, it is couched in langage that an average person of the writer's day might be expected to follow. These books were meant to be read by men and women without specialized training.

Since a large number of people, however, find many parts of the Bible difficult to understand, the task of interpretation is to allow light to shine in these dark places, so that books which were written for ordinary men and woman should become clear to them. Its function is to clarify, not to obscure. It should bridge the gap across the centuries, giving information which was taken for granted by the original readers but is unknown to most people in the modern age. Many of the problems of Bible reading are caused by the remoteness of its world from the present day and by our ignorance of the circumstances of its composition. Knowledge of the period when its books were written can provide important illumination in places where the meaning is not clear.

The zeal of scholars is not satisfied, however, with making clarifying comments about background or even with drawing out the meaning of the Scriptures for their original situation. As ingenious theories pile on top of each other, the inventiveness of experts can make the Bible more difficult to understand than it was before. The aim of scholarship is to make the Bible intelligible, but modern criticism in its attempt to clarify obscurities has constructed around the Scriptures a complex and intricate web of speculation from which the average reader retreats in bewilderment. In a large number of cases it is only speculation, and the basic message of a Scripture passage can be understood without it.

If the Bible is a collection of God-given documents, intended for all kinds of people, to show them God's will and to enlighten them about themselves, it must be interpreted intelligibly. The possibility that the authors of the biblical books used sources, altered them and rearranged them has to be faced. Honesty demands that this recognition be given; but a Christian interpretation must be intelligible as well as honest. It must not leave the reader trapped in a labyrinth of bewildering technicalities. Otherwise the Bible fails to be the medium through which truth is communicated. Effective interpretation enables people to understand the Bible. Honesty and intelligibility are characteristics to be expected of any account of the Scriptures which uses Jesus as interpreter.

2
Two Approaches to Jesus: Criticism and Faith

The Approach of Criticism

If Jesus is to be the interpreter of the Scriptures, it has to be decided who he is. The answer would appear to be simple. He was a man who lived in Palestine during the reigns of the Roman emperors Augustus and Tiberius. All that is needed, it would seem, is to make a historical inquiry into his activities. For many centuries it was assumed that the question could be answered by consulting the Bible, which was thought to contain a completely reliable record of his life and teaching. Four gospels are devoted to the theme of his life, claiming to give an account of his ministry and teaching, though none of them gives the whole story. According to the traditional view, they supplement each other, and the historian's task is to harmonize the four accounts and to produce a connected narrative from them. Scholars, who use this approach, have no doubt about the historical reliability of the gospels. They assume the records to be accurate and the scholar's task to be the explanation of background, the reconciliation of apparent inconsistencies, and the elucidation of the meaning of the gospels.

In recent years, however, the majority of investigators have discovered their task to be more complicated than their predecessors imagined. The possibility has been faced that the records may not be reliable. The infallibility, which has been previously credited to the Scriptures, is denied to them at the beginning of the investigation. The critic treats them as if they were as liable to error as other human compositions. They have been combed more ruthlessly and questioned more rigorously than any comparable documents. Christian commentators, eager to avoid the charge of being prejudiced in favour of them, have rushed into the fray and done their demolition work with remarkable zeal. Many of them have attempted to reconstruct the historical Jesus, a figure who, they claim, was imperfectly represented by the gospels. The clouds of interpretation which obscure him, they believe, must be penetrated in order to discover the real man, who, they expect, will reveal with a new vitality the essence of Christianity.

The Varieties of Historical Inquiry

The conclusions which they have reached are strong in imaginative invention but weak in ability to command general assent. The contradiction between the portraits of Jesus which have been painted suggests that no reliable conclusions can emerge from the enterprise. Hundreds of writings on the subject have appeared, ranging in their conclusions from a complete acceptance of the reliability of the gospel record to a total rejection of it. Rarely, if ever, in the history of human thought has the same basic evidence produced so diverse an assortment of conclusions.[1]

At one end of the spectrum are writers who claim that all four gospels are thoroughly reliable. They accept the veracity of the accounts of the virgin birth and resurrection of Jesus. They believe that he performed the miracles ascribed to him, healing the sick, feeding the hungry crowd, stilling the storm, and raising the dead to life. They claim that the gospels contain a thoroughly accurate record of his teaching. They argue that the New Testament portraits of him are faithful in most, if not all, of the details which they record.[2]

Probably the greatest number of scholars, however, in the twentieth century have given only partial acceptance to the reliability of the gospels. These scholars do not agree with each other about the extent of the material which is to be accepted as historically accurate. They have differing views about the miracle stories, some accepting only healing miracles—and not necessarily all of them—as historical, and others giving credence also to the accounts of nature-miracles like the feeding of the crowd and the stilling of the storm.

They differ in their verdicts about many of the stories which are not miraculous, including Jesus's triumphal entry into Jerusalem, the Last Supper, and the agony in Gethsemane. Some of them regard these narratives as reliable; others regard them as legendary. Stories with a clearly supernatural element in them, like the baptism of Jesus, his temptation, and his transfiguration, are treated as legends by some of these scholars, and as reliable, if slightly exaggerated, narratives by others. These critics vary also in their treatment of Jesus's teaching, some of them arguing that he made messianic claims for himself, others rejecting the idea. There is a wide variety of opinion among them about the reliability of the record of Jesus's ethical teaching. There is disagreement over the genuineness of his prophecies of his death and resurrection, and of the destruction of Jerusalem. There is dispute about the meaning and purpose of the parables. In their assessment of the general reliability of the gospel accounts of Jesus, these scholars are greatly divided. Some of them believe that, although the gospel writers have freely edited their material, they are basically trustworthy in the total impression which they give of Jesus's life and teaching. Other scholars believe that the gospels contain too much of their writers' own ideas to give a faithful impression of him. Between these points of view there ranges a great variety of opinion.[3]

Yet other critics have attempted to supply what they believe to be deficiencies of the gospels by introducing speculative reconstructions of events. By the use of their own ingenuity these scholars try to uncover facts which they think have been masked by the gospel writers. Although they do not entirely discount the historical value of the gospels, they believe them to be seriously misleading in many places. Such critics, therefore, provide their own theories about the true course of events and the real motives and plans of Jesus. While the gospels themselves teach that Jesus refused to take up arms and preached non-resistance to violence, some scholars depict him as a revolutionary leader who wanted an armed uprising against Rome.[4] Another claim is that he planned to stage a resurrection from a feigned death, and that his scheme was frustrated because he unexpectedly died.[5] Another intriguing piece of speculation, based on insecure foundations, is that Jesus was married, possibly to Mary Magdalene;[6] and even more intriguing is the suggestion that he was the founder of a secret, magical and libertine cult.[7] What all these theories have in common, in spite of their disagreements with each other, is their conviction that the truth is veiled by the gospels and that the scholar's task is to conjecture what lies behind the veil. The result is a fascinating amalgam of fiction and scholarship.

Some critics reject the evidence of the gospels as completely untrustworthy. They regard their contents as entirely legendary. They claim that there was no such man as Jesus of Nazareth, or that, if he did exist, the stories told about him are fictitious.[8] These writers explain the rise of Christianity in terms of cultic myths, and suggest that the stories were devised to convey secret religious teaching rather than to record events which actually happened. It is highly unlikely that records which can be dated back to within forty years of the events could be as completely fictitious as these writers claim them to be. Total scepticism about the historical reliability of the gospels is the least convincing verdict on them.

The Limitations of Criticism

Because of the remarkable variety of conclusions which have been reached, it would be absurd to speak of the assured results of scholarship in the quest of the historical Jesus. In different hands the tools of criticism have produced vastly different results. Whatever may have been the achievements of the critical method in other spheres of scholarly investigation, it has not achieved any resounding success in this one.

Champions of historical criticism claim that there is a large measure of agreement amongst scholars about certain aspects of Jesus's life and teaching. Most scholars, they maintain, believe that Jesus befriended sinners, provoked the opposition of scribes and Pharisees, gathered around him a group of disciples, and was arrested and crucified. The great majority of critics acknowledge that his was a ministry of preaching and healing. They agree that he taught about the Kingdom of God, emphasized the commandments of love, warned people of the danger of riches, and was responsible for at least some of the teaching ascribed to him in the Sermon on the

Mount. It is also generally acknowledged that he called men and women to a life of complete obedience to God.

Underlying these areas of consensus, however, are serious differences of opinion. There is disagreement whether Jesus believed the Kingdom of God to be present or future or a combination of both. There is debate about which sections of the Sermon on the Mount faithfully represent his teaching; some scholars reject the authenticity of the teaching about non-resistance, others that of the teaching about divorce, others that of the well-known saying, 'So whatever you wish that men would do to you, do so to them'.[9] There is disagreement also about the parables. Some scholars believe that Jesus was responsible for all of them. Others think that, although he uttered most of them, the gospel writers have sometimes distorted their meaning. Critics, however, who believe the gospels to veil the original form of the parables have not reached agreement about what Jesus actually said; nor have they attained any consensus about the meaning which he intended to convey when he told the parables. There is great disagreement also about the claims which he is said by the gospels to have made for himself. Scholars have not reached unanimity about the authenticity of the sayings in which he speaks of himself as uniquely related to God or as the fulfilment of messianic expectation. There is dispute also about the genuineness of the prophecies which he is supposed to have uttered about future events.

The extent of the disagreement is not surprising in view of the underlying areas of dispute. There is no unanimity about the order in which the gospels were written. Although the theory has long prevailed in Protestant circles that Mark's was the first of them to be written, this theory has its challengers. An alternative explanation, of great antiquity, is that Matthew's was the first of them. There is, moreover, no agreement about the extent to which the gospels made use of each other; nor is there any consensus about the sources which they used. Varied indeed are the theories about the extent to which the gospels made use of oral traditions and written documents.[10] The result in the case of all four gospels is that scholarly pronouncements are made about the contents, theology, and purpose of sources which may never have existed.

Yet another dispute concerns the degree of attention, which should be paid to John's Gospel in historical research into the life of Jesus. For many years historians based their conclusions mainly on the evidence afforded by the first three gospels. Their tendency was to regard John's Gospel as an important example of early Christian theology, but they believed it to be so saturated with theological interpretation that it was unreliable as historical evidence about Jesus. Even those scholars, who were highly sceptical about the trustworthiness of the first three gospels, relied on them more than on John's. In recent years, however, serious attention has been paid to the historical value of John's Gospel. Some scholars, while they hesitate to claim that it contains verbatim reports of the words of Jesus, have argued that it relies on early traditions. They have been ready to use it as serious evidence about Jesus's life and teaching.[11]

There is division of opinion also about the validity of the criteria that are employed to sift the authentic from the unauthentic records of Jesus's teaching. Some scholars work on the assumption that a saying is genuine unless there are overwhelming reasons for rejecting its authenticity. Others work on the assumption that a saying is genuine only when it could not conceivably have been uttered by anybody but Jesus. Between these extremes there is a great variety of viewpoints, some scholars working with a fixed set of criteria for assessing the reliability of the records, others improvising their criteria for each story or saying.[12]

The historical investigation of the gospels is riddled with disagreements, and inevitably so. There is not the evidence available to decide with certainty about the order in which the gospels were written or about their dependence on each other. Since no certain sources of the gospels can be traced, any theories about sources must inevitably remain in the realm of conjecture. As for the criteria for determining the genuineness of sayings, their selection is a highly subjective affair. There is no self-evident procedure for choosing criteria, and the selection depends to a great extent on the degree of scepticism possessed by the scholar who chooses them.

There are some aspects of the biblical Jesus which are beyond the scope of historical investigation. Biblical criticism cannot prove or disprove that Jesus rose from the dead. It cannot verify the reports of the event with certainty. Even though it may detect inconsistencies between the gospel accounts of the resurrection, it cannot reach a reliable verdict on the fundamental question whether he actually came to life again; nor can it prove or disprove that he stilled a storm, miraculously fed a crowd, and brought dead people back to life. There is no proof that it is impossible for these events to occur, especially if the agent is the unique Son of God. Under normal circumstances, if the agent was an ordinary person, it would be a natural reaction to be doubtful about the accuracy of the reports of these events, but those, who accept Jesus as uniquely related to God, do not regard these as normal circumstances; and historical criticism is not equipped to make a final decision on this question.

It is highly misleading to speak of the sure and certain results of scholarship in the quest for the historical Jesus. The discipline of critical scholarship is not able to reach anywhere near certainty in its investigations into the matter. Rich and instructive though its discoveries may be in other areas, it has failed here to reach its goal. Unfortunately the impression is often given that the findings of this or that particular scholar have a certainty which they do not possess. Assumptions which are in fact dogmatic are set forth as if they were the product of a foolproof process of scientific reasoning; but if scholarship is to be consistently critical, it should refrain from giving the impression that its conclusions are more certain than they really are.

A critical investigation into the life of Jesus is not superfluous. It provides important background information about the times in which he lived, and clarifies the meaning of the gospel accounts of his life and teaching. It offers theories about the sources of biblical writings and about the identity of their authors. It discusses the purposes for which the books were written, and the circumstances of their composition; but it cannot decide whether supernatural events occurred or not. It cannot determine the extent to which the sayings ascribed to Jesus faithfully convey the essentials of his teaching. It can neither prove nor disprove that he is the unique divine person whom the New Testament writers claim him to be. There is indeed a possibility, if only a theoretical one, that critical investigation of the gospels could undermine the credibility of the Christian message. If

Jesus could be shown to have practised the very vices which he condemned, to have been a thief or murderer or an adulterer or a self-righteous bigot, the compelling power of his appeal would be broken. Since Christianity claims to be founded on fact, the strength of its message would be shattered if Jesus had been a rogue and a hypocrite. In reality, however, he has not been discredited in this way. Biblical criticism has not disproved the reliability of the gospel accounts of him any more than it has conclusively proved it.

The Approach of Faith

It is possible to discover Jesus in a vastly different way from that of the inconclusive probings of historical research. He can be discovered through the way of faith, which accepts the New Testament accounts of him as authentic portraits. When this approach to him is used, Jesus is not the inaccessible, tantalizing goal of an endless process of historical inquiry. He is to be found in the biblical portraits of him, which are accessible to anyone who reads the New Testament. It is this biblical Jesus, who is the authentic Christian interpreter of the Bible.[13]

Any attempt to look at the Scriptures with him as guide must be based on a trust in the New Testament writers as faithful witnessess to him. Provided biblical criticism has found no overwhelming reason for rejecting the authenticity of the gospel impressions of Jesus, faith can accept him, not as an inspiring myth or legend, but as a man who really lived the kind of life depicted in the gospels. The very inconclusiveness of historical research leaves the door open for faith. The fact that some scholars, having subjected the gospels to critical examination, conclude that these portraits of Jesus are credible, shows that faith is not capricious. Faith, however, does not depend on the support of any given percentage of critics, whether it be ninety or seventy or fifty or thirty or ten per cent, but is a direct response to the intrinsic worth and the powerful appeal of the biblical portraits of Jesus.

The object of this faith is described in this book as the 'biblical Jesus' rather than the 'biblical Christ'.[14] The reason for this preference is the need to affirm the identity of Jesus of Nazareth with the Christ of the early Church's preaching. Too often the word 'Christ' is used with such ambiguity that he is not clearly regarded as one and the same person as Jesus of Nazareth. Many people claim to believe in Christ without believing that Jesus is the Christ or that the New Testament writers have given faithful portraits of him; but Christian faith is faith in Jesus as the Christ. It is a trust in the biblical witnesses to him. These biblical witnesses do not suppose themselves to be setting forth a fiction. They believe that Jesus really was the kind of man whom they portray, and that he really rose from the dead. Faith, venturing beyond the uncertainties of historical criticism, and responding to the powerful claim of the writings themselves, recognizes the biblical Jesus to be the Christ whom the early Church preached as Lord. It also recognizes him to be the Jesus who actually lived and was crucified, who rose from the dead and is alive today. It is this Jesus who provides the distinctively Christian interpretation of the Scriptures.

3
The Biblical Jesus:
The Gospels and the Acts

Impressions of Jesus

Jesus the interpreter of the Bible is Jesus as he is depicted in the Bible itself. He is to be found in the portraits of him given by the New Testament writers. By far the most vivid and detailed of these portraits are provided by the gospels. While all the writings of the New Testament testify to his divinity and his transforming power, it is the gospels which supply the clearest account of the kind of man he was and the kind of teaching he gave.

It is in terms of general impressions rather than comprehensiveness of information that the biblical portraits of Jesus are to be understood. The gospel writers recorded events not merely to affirm that Jesus took part in them, but also to convey the impression which Jesus made on men and women. Mark's Gospel, for example, gives a representative selection of the miracles of Jesus: the stilling of a storm, the walking on the water, the feeding of a crowd in Jewish territory, the feeding of another crowd in Gentile territory, the healings of a leper, a paralytic, a dumb boy, an epileptic boy, a girl who was apparently dead, a woman with a hemorrhage, a man with a withered hand, a man with an unclean spirit, a demoniac who was possessed by a multitude of demons, and two healings of blind men.[1] Whether Mark selected them instinctively or deliberately, he succeeded in giving a representative impression of Jesus's activities. He did not attempt to record every action which Jesus performed. His aim was not to give a full-scale biography of him, but to tell his readers who Jesus was and what he was like. The gospels were

designed to show the kind of person Jesus was rather than to produce a list of his achievements. They present him in a variety of
situations and give a selection of his teaching. They depict him as
the revealer of God, the saviour of men and women, the example
and teacher for his followers. They convey impressions of him, besides recording incidents in which he participated.

Impressions reveal more about an individual than do the mere
chronicles of sayings and activities. A historian who only records
events fails to convey their true impact and leaves a collection of
irrelevant details. While the total impact of a person is made over a
period of many months and years, the reader of a history or biography must receive the impact within a few pages. A mere record or
summary of events will not in itself convey the impact. The selection of material and the style of its presentation helps to give the
total impression of a person.

The gospels do not contain detailed historical documentation,
according to modern standards of judgement, but provide evidence
of the impression which Jesus made on men and women. They are
not intended to give the full details of his life and teaching. By a
representative selection of stories and sayings they attempt to present him as he strikes the writers. Recent scholarship has put great
emphasis on the gospel writers as theologians. Attention has long
been given to this aspect of John's Gospel. Scholars now attempt
also to delineate the theologies of Matthew, Mark and Luke. A
great deal of research has been done in this area.[2] It confirms the
belief that the gospel writers intended to convey an overall impression of Jesus rather than to give a full-scale biography of him. The
gospels present testimonies to Jesus, differing in detail and varying
in emphasis, yet agreeing in their conviction that Jesus gives new
life to those who trust in him. The writers are not primarily seeking
to give an exhaustive account of events but to awaken or confirm
faith in Christ. They desire the readers to receive the same impact
from Jesus as they themselves have experienced, and to follow him
as they have done.

The First Three Gospels and the Acts of the Apostles

Impressions of Jesus are based chiefly on the four gospels, because they give the clearest and most detailed portraits of him.

Among the gospels there is the greatest amount of accord between Matthew, Mark and Luke; and these will be considered together. It is appropriate also to examine the Acts of the Apostles at the same time, since it is the work of the author of Luke's Gospel. Although the portraits given by these three writers do not completely coincide, there is a large amount of agreement between them.

They agree that Jesus is *uniquely related to God.* All of them describe him as the Son of God and record the special way in which he was addressed by God at his baptism and transfiguration.[3] All of them affirm that he is risen from the dead.[4] Matthew and Luke include stories of his miraculous birth, when he was conceived by the Spirit.[5] All of them describe him as one who pronounced forgiveness, a function which in the Jewish world was usually reserved for God.[6] All of them tell the story of the stilling of a storm in such a way as to imply his divinity.[7] In these ways the gospels indicate that he was uniquely related to God.

There is agreement between these gospel writers that Jesus is the *unique revealer of God.* Matthew and Luke record the saying that knowledge of the Father is limited to those to whom the Son chooses to reveal him.[8] At Jesus's transfiguration, according to all three of these gospels, God commands the disciples to listen to Jesus, who is his Son.[9] And in all three gospels Jesus indicates that his disciples have received the secrets of the Kingdom.[10] The common theme of these passages is that Jesus uniquely reveals God.

These writers agree that Jesus is the *saviour.* Even though they do not all actually use the word 'saviour', they all indicate that he is the bringer of salvation, which includes both physical healing and the forgiveness of sins. As well as restoring the sick and handicapped, he enables people to be saved from their sins.[11] The gospels also make it clear that his death is an integral part of his work of salvation. According to Mark and Matthew he is the Son of man who came to give his life a ransom for many; and the blood which he shed was the blood of the covenant, an assertion which implies that his death inaugurated a new covenant between God and the human race.[12] In Luke's Gospel also the idea is found that his death ratifies the new covenant, although it is uncertain that these words were in the earliest text of the gospel.[13] The Acts of the Apostles records the statement that the Church was purchased with Jesus's blood. Both Luke and Acts regard him as the fulfilment of the prophecy of a Suffering Servant who will give his life for the people.[14] Moreover, Luke regards the whole of Jesus's ministry as an event which makes possible the gift of the Spirit. Jesus was the bringer of salvation through the work which he did, reaching its climax in his death, resurrection and ascension, followed by the outpouring of the Spirit at Pentecost.[15] But Jesus is not just concerned with salvation from sickness and from sins in this present life. He speaks of a future salvation. Those who lose their lives for his sake will save them. Those who endure to the end will be saved. Such is the message of all three of these writers.[16]

These gospels concur in their account of Jesus's *personal characteristics.* They depict him as a man of determined purpose, utterly obedient to God even to the point of death,[17] strong in criticism of hypocrisy and injustice,[18] ready to befriend the outcasts and sinners,[19] showing love and compassion to those who were in need.[20] He is depicted as peaceful yet strong, obviously confident of his vocation and his relationship to God.[21] He is portrayed as a man without material wealth, who lives a life of simplicity[22] but not of utter asceticism, a man who shares in the festivities of everyday life.[23] He is subject to temptation but always resists it. He refuses the invitation to yield himself to the devil to win political power. He will not seek easy success by spectacular gimmicks,[24] resists the temptation to avoid the pain and agony of death.[25] In his general bearing he is seen as a man of incomparable authority in both his teaching and his works of healing.[26] There are differences of emphasis in these writings, and not exactly the same portrait is to be found in all of them. But their overall picture of Jesus is recognizably that of the same man. He has distinctive characteristics which emerge in all three of these gospels.

The portraits of Jesus as a *teacher* are similar in these writings. The Kingdom of God is the central theme of his teaching in all of them. They also agree that Jesus made great claims about himself. They depict him as one who regarded himself as Son of God and Son of man,[27] showed reluctance to admit that he was Messiah[28] and prophesied his own suffering, death and resurrection.[29] They agree that he called on God as Father[30] and stressed God's mercy to sinners and also God's judgement on them. They agree that he proclaimed the coming of the Kingdom of God, and appealed to men and women to repent of their sins.[31] They agree that he regarded love for God and love for neighbour as the first of all the commandments.[32] They record his emphasis on service to one another, and his call to be ready to sacrifice everything, wealth and even life, for the sake of the gospel.[33] They speak of his teaching about the sanctity of marriage and his opposition to divorce. They concur that he refrained from violent revolution and uttered warnings against the dangers of wealth.[34] They record his teaching about inner purity, about the importance of thoughts and motives by contrast with outward show. They agree that he expected a resurrection of the dead at the last day and a final judgement which he himself would inaugurate.[35] They contain accounts of his emphasis on the importance of prayer, and although they do not all include his instruction that the celebration of the Last Supper should be perpetuated, they all record his use on the occasion of liturgical language which gives the impression of the inauguration of a solemn rite.[36]

The differences which can be found between these portraits of Jesus as teacher are secondary. The main impression is one of agreement. For example, although it is only in Matthew and Luke that Jesus asserts that the Kingdom of God has already come,[37] the absence of a clear reference to the presence of the Kingdom in Mark should not be allowed to obscure that gospel's emphasis on Jesus's offer of new life here and now. For Mark, as for the other gospels, Jesus's call to discipleship is a summons to an immediate change of life.[38]

Another matter in which the differences should not be allowed to obscure the agreement is divorce. According to Matthew, Jesus permits divorce only on the grounds of unchastity, which presumably means adultery.[39] According to Mark and Luke, he will not sanction divorce for any reason.[40] Even this difference is one of detail, not of principle. All three gospels agree that he upheld the lifelong nature of marriage. The differences, which exist between them, are small in comparison with the large measure of agreement that they display.

There are differences also in the accounts of Jesus's words at the Last Supper. Only Luke mentions Jesus's command to repeat the celebration, and not all early manuscripts are agreed that the command was in Luke's original text, although it is included by Paul in his account of the incident. While Mark and Matthew include words which clearly refer to the sacrificial aspect of Jesus's death, the early manuscripts do not all include this theme in Luke's account, but in spite of these differences there is much agreement. All three gospels describe a rite involving the use of bread and wine, which is related to the death of Jesus Christ. All of them see it as a foretaste of a future feast in God's Kingdom.[41]

Since these gospels are written by different authors, it is only to be expected that there will be differences of emphasis. Matthew gives more detailed ethical teaching than do the others. He records more teaching about the Church and more about the Last Judgement. Luke lays more stress on Jesus's message of mercy and forgiveness, on the preaching of the gospel to all men and women, on the perils of worldly wealth, and on the importance of prayer; but this is a case of varieties of emphasis. The gospels do not disagree with each other on these matters.

Jesus's function as *example* is another aspect of the impression conveyed by these writings. All of them record how he tells his disciples to be servants to others, just as he himself is a servant. They include his appeal to them to take up their crosses and follow him.[42] In Matthew's Gospel he says that 'it is enough for the disciple to be like his teacher, and the servant like his master'.[43] The pattern of life described in the Sermon on the Mount is exemplified by Jesus himself. His function as example is to be discerned even in the use of a word like 'meek', which occurs in Matthew with reference to both Jesus and his disciples. Jesus says of himself, 'I am meek and lowly in heart', and to his followers he gives the assurance 'Blessed are the meek'.[44] Luke's writings have distinctive ways of presenting Jesus as the example. Stephen's words at the moment of his death, his prayer for the forgiveness of his murderers, and his committal of his spirit to God, are similar to the words of Jesus on the cross as recorded by Luke.[45] Paul's determination to go to Jerusalem at the end of his third missionary journey and his expectation of persecution and death is another instance of the correspondence between the life of a follower of Jesus and that of Jesus himself. It reflects the mood ascribed by Luke to Jesus as he made his last journey to Jerusalem.[46] Although the writers have different ways of conveying the point, they are in complete agreement that Jesus set an example to be followed.

The first three gospels and the Acts also emphasize *the identity of Jesus with the risen Christ.* Each of them contains an account of the resurrection,[47] and there is no doubt that Jesus is the man who has risen. They also indicate that the risen Christ is *the living Christ.* They declare that he is seated at the right hand of God.[48] Luke's writings depict him as the giver of the Spirit, enabling people to preach, speak in tongues, bear witness under persecution, and reach agreement over difficult and divisive issues.[49] Mark does not give as full an account of the Spirit's activity as does Luke; but in Mark, as in the other gospels, Jesus is said to be the one who will baptize with the Spirit, and the Spirit is said to enable Jesus's followers to speak in time of persecution.[50] Besides making the same points as Mark does about the Spirit, Matthew includes sayings, which speak of the continuing presence of Jesus with his disciples after the resurrection appearances have ended: where two or three are gathered together in his name, he is in their midst; he is with them always, to the end of the age.[51] There is no clear distinction here between the ever-present Christ and the Holy Spirit. Luke's writings speak of the Spirit more than do the others, but all three writers speak of the continuing divine presence in the lives of Jesus's followers, whether they describe it in terms of the Spirit or of Christ. The risen Christ is also *the coming Christ.* All three of these writers expect his return at the end of the age. He will come to gather the elect and to pass judgement on men and women.[52] Jesus, who rose from the dead and is now reigning with God, will be active in the final triumph of God.

The similarity between the portraits of Jesus in the writings of Mark, Matthew and Luke is usually explained by theories about sources which they used. If Mark's Gospel was the first to be written, then Matthew and Luke used Mark together with additional source material. If Matthew's was the first to be written, then Mark and Luke used Matthew. Although, however, these theories give explanations of the existence of similarities between the gospels, they do not explain why the gospel writers selected the particular material which they contain. Out of the available sources each writer chose the material which he believed to be appropriate for his purpose. Each of them was responsible for the final selection which he made, however much he made use of sources. It is the writer himself who, by the nature of his selection, determines the character of the portrait of Jesus which emerges. Each of them uses different combinations of material. Each is giving his own impression of Jesus. But different though the impressions may be in detail, there is a striking amount of agreement between them in the themes which have been outlined.

It is a very speculative enterprise to attempt to go behind the Jesus of the gospels to the Jesus of the sources which the writers may have used. It is highly debatable what these sources were. It is not known to what extent they were written and to what extent they were oral. Any attempt to substitute the portraits of Jesus in these hypothetical sources for the portraits given by the gospels is a retreat from evidence which is available to evidence which is not available. By contrast with the uncertainty which surrounds the question of sources, there is the certainty that the writers of the gospels were responsible for the selection of the material which they used. The Jesus of the gospels is Jesus as he made his impact on these writers. He is Jesus as he was understood by them, not by a compiler of an unknown source which may never have existed.

John's Gospel

Although the portrait of Jesus given by John's Gospel has noticeable differences from those in the others, it has much in common with them, and presents the same central themes as they do. Like the other three gospels, John's depicts Jesus as *uniquely related to God.* It is in fact much more explicit about this uniqueness than the other gospels. It represents him as claiming to be Son of God with a greater openness than they do.[53] It even affirms that he was alive before the time of Abraham.[54] The assertion that in Jesus 'the Word became flesh' indicates that he was the incarnation of the divine Word that was active in the creation of the world.[55] The variety of sayings which begin with the words 'I am', such as 'I am the bread of life' and 'I am the light of the world' imply a close link between Jesus and God, who in the Old Testament is revealed as 'I am' and 'I am he'.[56] Thomas's confession of Jesus as 'My Lord and my God!'[57] affirms that he is divine. In all these ways John's Gospel, even more emphatically than the other three, presents the theme that Jesus has a unique relationship to God.

John's Gospel agrees with the other three in portraying Jesus as the *unique revealer of God*. 'No one has ever seen God'; it asserts, 'the only Son, who is in the bosom of the Father, he has made him known'.[58] 'He who has seen me', says Jesus, 'has seen the Father'.[59] The very message of Jesus has been given to him by God. 'The Father who sent me', he says, 'has himself given me commandment what to say and what to speak'.[60] Indeed it is in this gospel that the theme of Jesus as the revealer of God can be discerned even more clearly than in the others.

There is no uncertainty about the prominence in this gospel of the theme that Jesus is *saviour*. He is explicitly described as 'the saviour' and himself asserts that his mission is to save rather than to condemn.[61] His sacrificial death is the means of liberating men and women from the dominion of sin. He is the Lamb of God who 'takes away the sin of the world', the good shepherd who died for the sheep.[62] While he saves people from sin and death, enabling them to enjoy eternal life,[63] he also gives physical salvation through his miracles. He gives bread to the hungry crowd. He heals the lame and the blind. He brings the dead back to life.[64] But these acts of physical salvation are signs also of his power to give eternal salvation. Not only does he provide physical bread; he himself, in a spiritual sense, is the bread of life.[65] Not only does he give physical sight to the blind; in a spiritual sense he is the light of the world.[66] Not only does he raise up the dead man, Lazarus, to longer life on earth; he offers men and women eternal life, and promises to raise them up at the last day.[67]

In its account of the *personal characteristics* of Jesus, John's Gospel has much in common with the others. Like them it depicts Jesus as a man of strong purpose, ready to face death in obedience to God's will.[68] It shows him as the opponent of legalistic Jews.[69] While it never actually mentions his friendship with tax-collectors and sinners, it records his encounter with a Samaritan woman of doubtful reputation.[70] He heals the sick, as he does in the other gospels. Even though there is no mention in John's Gospel of an exorcism, there is evidence enough of his activity as a healer. The general impression is that he was a man of inner peace, and at the same time a man of courage and power. He showed love and compassion for others. He was ready to share in festivities.[71] Although there is no temptation story in John's Gospel, he is said to have resisted the offer of political kingship, and to have dismissed from his mind the thought that he might escape from crucifixion.[72] In all these ways the portrait of Jesus in John's Gospel is similar to those in the others.

It has been argued that John's Gospel fails to depict a truly human Jesus, but shows him as a manifestation of divine glory rather than a real human being. It is contended that the gospel has been influenced by Docetism, a type of thought which claimed either that Jesus only appeared to be human or that the divine Christ was not truly united with the human Jesus.[73] Such accounts of him, however, are inconsistent with the portrait of him in John's Gospel with its assertion that Jesus was the Word made flesh.[74] It was the gospel's intention to describe Jesus as a real man of flesh and blood, who was capable of human feelings like weariness, thirst and inner anguish.[75] John's portrait of Jesus is fundamentally anti-Docetic.

The portrait of Jesus as *teacher* in John's Gospel differs from those in the other gospels in important respects. Most of its account of his teaching concerns his own relationship to God, and describes his function as saviour, judge, revealer of God, and giver of eternal life. Jesus is portrayed as speaking of himself more openly and frequently than in the other gospels. He makes some of the same claims as in the others. He speaks of himself as Son of man and Son of God,[76] and only admits rarely that he is Messiah.[77] The points, however, where John's Gospel goes much further than the others are its accounts of Jesus's claim to have existed before Abraham,[78] of his assertion that he is one with the Father,[79] and of his statement that he will raise up the dead at the last day.[80] John is in agreement with the other gospels in depicting Jesus as one who makes great claims for himself. But in John the claims are more far-reaching than in the other gospels.

The ethical teaching of John's Gospel differs from that of the others in its concentration on general exhortations to the exclusion of the particular. John gives a central place to the commandment of love,[81] but is silent about details of conduct. It does not follow, however, that this gospel regards the details as irrelevant. It shows an awareness of the existence of more than one commandment. 'If you love me,' says Jesus, 'you will keep my commandments'.[82] Since he promises that the Spirit will remind his disciples of all that he has taught them, [83] it is legitimate to conclude that a body of teaching is presupposed which is not included in the gospel.

Whatever these other commandments may have been, John's portrait of Jesus is thoroughly consistent with the pattern of life set forth in Matthew's Gospel in the Sermon on the Mount, with its stress on love, meekness, and purity of heart. It is also in agreement with the other gospels when it depicts Jesus as refusing to bring about God's will by force of arms or to offer violent resistance to his persecutors.[84] John's Gospel also affirms that Jesus was primarily concerned to give spiritual rather than material blessings. The bread of life was more important than ordinary food and drink.[85] This attitude is similar to that of Jesus in the other gospels, where he tells men and women to lay up treasure for themselves in heaven rather than on earth.[86] Although no specific teaching about marriage and divorce is found in John's Gospel, high standards for marriage are reflected in its account of Jesus's conversation with a Samaritan woman.[87] In spite of the absence of detailed ethical instructions John's portrait of Jesus indicates agreement with some of the particular themes of his teaching reported in the other gospels.

John's Gospel has been criticized for presenting the commandment of love only in terms of loving one another,[88] as though it were limited to relationships between the followers of Jesus and did not include relationships with non-Christians. This is a misleading account of the gospel's teaching. Because it was written for a situation in which the Church was threatened with division, it lays an emphasis on harmony and love within the Christian community. It does not exclude the idea that love extends beyond these limits, but asserts that God loved the world so much that he sent his Son to die for it.[89] It has a clear conception of the universal mission of the Church. Jesus promises to bring into the Church those who are not of this fold, that is, not of the Jewish nation. And he prays for those who have not yet believed in him, asserting that they are loved by God.[90] While the theme of love of enemies is not introduced, the idea of a love that extends beyond the boundaries of the Church is implicit in John's Gospel.

Like the other gospels, John's depicts Jesus as teaching the importance of prayer. The emphasis in John on worship in Spirit and in truth corresponds to the emphasis in Matthew on the importance of inner attitude in prayer; and although John's Gospel does not describe the institution of the Lord's Supper, it records words of Jesus about eating his flesh and drinking his blood which are obviously concerned with the subject.[91]

A further emphasis which John's Gospel shares with the others is its account of Jesus as the *example* which people are to follow. His disciples are exhorted to love one another as Jesus has loved them, and to wash one another's feet as he has washed theirs.[92] But it is not just as an example that Jesus is set forward. He is the one who dwells in his disciples, as they also dwell in him.[93] He is in fact the very life which nurtures them.[94]

John's Gospel is like the others in stressing *the identity of Jesus with the risen Christ.*[95] Like them it portrays him as *the living Christ.* He is with the Father in glory. He is the giver of the Spirit, and dwells in those who believe in him. Indeed this gospel puts special emphasis on the activity of the Spirit. It is through the Spirit that men and women can be born again. The Spirit guides them into all truth. The Spirit reminds them of his teaching, and bears witness to him. When he breathes the Spirit on his disciples after his resurrection, it is implied that a new creation is taking place. The Spirit is not separated from Christ himself; the Spirit is sent by him, and there is no indication that there is any clear division between the activity of the indwelling Spirit and the activity of the indwelling Christ.[96] As well as being the living and indwelling Christ, however, Jesus is also *the coming Christ.* He is the Son of man whose voice the dead will hear at the Last Judgement, and who will raise men and women up at the last day.[97] Although John's Gospel lays more emphasis on the activity of Christ as the giver of eternal life in the present than in the future, it has a clear and sure place in its message for his activity in the future.

It is obvious that there are important differences between John's Gospel and the other three: differences of content and emphasis, differences in the sequence of events, and even differences of precise dating. [98] However, in its overall impression of Jesus the Gospel of John shows a large measure of agreement with the others, even though the particular incidents and teachings recorded are not often the same. The main themes which have been outlined are common to all four gospels. Jesus, they all agree, is uniquely related to God, uniquely reveals God, and is the saviour. He is a man with distinctive characteristics, reflected in all of these gospels. He is also the teacher and the example. He is the risen Christ, who is alive in the present and will come again in the future. Each of the gospel writers looks at Jesus from a different angle. But the face which they depict is the face of the same man. There are four portraits, but one Jesus.

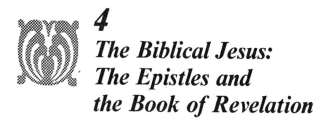

4
The Biblical Jesus:
The Epistles and
the Book of Revelation

Paul's Letters

The letters of Paul do not give as detailed an impression of Jesus as do the gospels. A letter is not likely to do this as fully as a gospel, because it does not contain an account of the actions and teaching of Jesus. Nevertheless, Paul conveys an impression of Jesus which is in basic agreement with those given by Mark, Matthew, Luke and John.

Paul teaches that Jesus is *uniquely related to God.* He affirms that Christ existed before his physical birth, and even asserts that he was active in the creation of the universe.[1] He declares that Jesus Christ is Son of God, and Lord,[2] and that before his coming to earth he was on an equality with God.[3] Some of Paul's language could be interpreted as suggesting a subordination of Christ to God the Father,[4] but of the uniqueness of the relationship between the two there is no doubt whatever.

In Paul's writings Jesus emerges as *the unique revealer of God.* It was 'through a revelation of Jesus Christ'[5] that Paul received the gospel. God has shown his love for us through the death of Jesus.[6] He has shone in our hearts 'to give the light of the knowledge of the glory of God in the face of Christ'.[7] He has 'set forth' his purpose in Christ,[8] who is the one in whom are hid 'all the treasures of wisdom and knowledge'.[9]

There is evidence enough that Paul regarded Jesus as *saviour.* He is the saviour who is awaited from heaven, the saviour of the Church.[10] It is through faith in him that men and women can be

justified by the grace of God,[11] and those who build on him as a
foundation will obtain salvation at the last day.[12] Salvation is a present blessing and a future hope. The present salvation is made possible through Jesus's death, which is understood in sacrificial terms.
The future salvation takes place at the coming of Christ on the last
day.

Paul does not lay the same emphasis as do the gospel writers on
the personal characteristics of Jesus. Since his references to Jesus's
life are concerned mainly with his crucifixion and resurrection, it is
sometimes argued that he was not interested in the earthly Jesus.[13]
Such a verdict is far from the truth. It is not only the final events in
Jesus's life which are important for Paul. His allusions to the personal characteristics of Jesus presuppose a vivid impression of him,
which Paul does not need to reproduce fully in his letters because
the purpose of his writing does not demand it. He speaks of the way
in which Jesus humbled himself and showed obedience to God.[14] He
speaks of the meekness and gentleness of Christ.[15] Even though he
does not paint a detailed portrait, a general impression of Jesus
emerges from his letters which is in agreement with those in the
gospels.

In Paul's letters Jesus is depicted as *teacher.* There are specific
references to his institution of the Lord's Supper and to his teaching
about divorce.[16] Several of Paul's ethical exhortations are remarka-
bly similar both in language and meaning to the gospels' account of
the teaching of Jesus. Like Jesus, he stresses the centrality of the law
of love and tells people to refrain from violence.[17] Like Jesus, he
exhorts them to obedience and humility.[18] Like Jesus, he counsels
indifference to worldly wealth.[19] Even though he does not often al-
lude explicitly to the sayings of Jesus, he seems to presuppose an
impression of Jesus's teaching which is consistent with that of the
gospels. Moreover, he attaches special importance to the authority
of Jesus's words, contrasting that 'I' say with what the 'Lord' says.[20]
The way in which he refers to Jesus's teaching is evidence of its
importance for him.

Paul also conveys an impression of Jesus as an *example.* His
humility and his obedience even to the point of death are commended as a pattern to be followed.[21] His love for the Church is a

model of the love which husbands should show to their wives.[22] His lack of concern to please himself and his readiness to welcome others are commended as virtues to be imitated.[23] The idea of example merges into that of union with Christ, so that the believer participates in Christ's sufferings and shares in his death and resurrection.[24] Whether it is expressed in terms of example or of union, Jesus's life is held up as a pattern for men and women.

In unambiguous terms Paul asserts that Jesus, who died and was buried, is the Christ who was raised on the third day.[25] *The identity of Jesus with the risen Christ* is a central theme for Paul; and the risen Christ is *the living Christ,* who is at the right hand of God.[26] Paul is in Christ, and Christ is in Paul. Indeed all things have their existence through Christ.[27] The activity of the living Christ is also to be discerned in the work of the Spirit. No New Testament writer has richer or fuller teaching about the Spirit than Paul. He speaks of the various gifts of the Spirit by which men and women are enabled to prophesy, perform miracles, heal the sick, speak in tongues, and fulfil the varied ministries of the Church, as well as to have wisdom and knowledge about spiritual things.[28] He also speaks of the fruit of the Spirit, which includes love, joy, peace, patience, kindness and other similar gifts.[29] The Spirit is not just responsible for particular ministries in the Church or particular moments of heightened religious experience. The Spirit bears fruit in a life of a quality which is clearly that exemplified by Jesus Christ himself. Just as Paul can speak of being in Christ, so he can speak of being in the Spirit. Just as he can speak of Christ being in him, so he can speak of the Spirit being in him. For Paul the Spirit is 'the Spirit of Christ'.[30] The presence of the Spirit cannot be separated from the presence of the living Christ. This same living Christ is also *the coming Christ,* who will appear at the last day when the dead are raised and judgement takes place,[31] and the Spirit functions as a guarantee of the future that the coming Christ will bring.[32] The presence of the Spirit is a divine pledge that the future belongs to Jesus Christ.

Even though Paul has not written a gospel and mentions only a few details of the life and teaching of Jesus, he presupposes an impression of Jesus which is similar to those given by the gospels. Like the gospels, he stresses the uniqueness of Jesus's relationship to God and of his function as the revealer of God. Like them, he emphasizes Jesus's function as saviour and example. Like them, he affirms the identity of Jesus with the risen Christ, who is also the living Christ and the Christ to come. Jesus's personal characteristics are not described in the same detail by Paul as by the gospels, but, in so far as Paul mentions them, they are consistent with the picture presented by the gospels. The teaching of Jesus is rarely alluded to by Paul, but when it is mentioned, it is in agreement with the gospel record, as are most of the emphases in Paul's ethical teaching.[33]

The Letter to the Hebrews

Most of these themes appear also in the Letter to the Hebrews, a work which, it is generally recognized, was not written by Paul. No clearer assertion of the belief that Jesus is *uniquely related to God* can be found than the opening paragraph of this letter with its description of him as 'the heir of all things', the agent in the creation of the world, the one who bears the stamp of God's nature and is superior to the angels.[34] This letter describes him as the *unique revealer of God.* It asserts that God, who spoke through the Hebrew prophets, has spoken 'in these last days' through a Son.[35] Jesus is also the *saviour,* who made purification for sins, is 'the source of eternal salvation to all who obey him', and will appear a second time 'to save those who are eagerly waiting for him', [36] Some of his *personal characteristics* are emphasized in the letter. He was a man of godly fear and faith.[37] He was beset by weakness and temptation, and had to learn obedience.[38] There is reference also to him as an *example.* He is the author and perfecter of faith, to whom Christians look as they run life's race.[39] His suffering outside the gate of Jerusalem is set forward as a pattern for those who bear abuse for his sake.[40] The letter asserts his identity *with the risen Christ.* By its emphasis on his place at the right hand of God, it gives recognition to Jesus as the risen one.[41] It identifies the risen, enthroned Jesus with the *living Christ,* who ministers in the heavenly sanctuary where he makes intercession for us,[42] and it regards him as the *coming Christ* who will appear a second time to bring salvation to those who wait for him.[43]

The theme of Jesus as teacher is not explicitly stated in this letter; but while there is no specific reference to his words, the instructions which the letter gives about hospitality to strangers, care for prisoners, the sanctity of marriage and the avoidance of the love of money are thoroughly consistent with the gospel accounts of Jesus's teaching.[44]

Other Writings

In varying degree the other New Testament writings give support to the themes which have been mentioned. They all stress his unique relationship to God, by describing him as Son of God or Lord.[45] Some of them speak of his work as the unique revelation of God. The First Letter of John describes him as the manifestation of eternal life, and the Book of Revelation stresses his function as revealer of future events, not through the medium of his earthly life but through his spiritual communication with John who receives the revelation.[46] Most of these writings mention his function as the bringer of both present and future salvation.[47] His personal characteristics are mentioned by some of them. The First Letter of Peter speaks of his readiness to suffer silently and his absence of guile. The Book of Revelation speaks of him as the faithful witness.[48] His function as example also is mentioned by the First Letter of Peter when it describes his suffering.[49] Most of these books assert his identity with the risen Christ, and depict him as both the living Christ and the future Christ.[50] Even the Letter of James, which only refers to him twice by name, describes him as the Lord of glory and speaks of the coming of the Lord.[51]

As for the teaching of Jesus, these writings commend standards of conduct consistent with it. They emphasize love of neighbour; they warn about the danger of riches and temptations to immorality; they stress the importance of humility and endurance.[52] There are differences of emphasis among these writings. The Book of Revelation, for example, devotes special attention to the theme of judgement; and if some of its statements are taken literally, they do not easily harmonize with the overall New Testament impression of Jesus. But for the most part these writings present teaching which is in accord with the gospel portraits of him.

A Consensus

The first three gospels produce a consensus in their impressions of Jesus. The seven themes which have been discussed are clearly found there: 1. He is uniquely related to God; 2. He is the unique revealer of God; 3. He is the saviour; 4. He has clearly recognizable personal characteristics; 5. He is a teacher with a distinctive message to convey; 6. He is an example to be followed; 7. He is identified with the risen Christ, who is also the living and the coming Christ.

John's Gospel confirms the impression given by these other three. While there are striking differences between this gospel and the others, it includes the seven themes mentioned. In presenting the fifth theme, that of Jesus's function as teacher, it does not give the same detailed instruction about conduct as do the other gospels, and it lays greater emphasis on his teaching about himself, but these are differences of emphasis. All seven themes are present in John's Gospel. It gives a different portrait of Jesus from those found in the other gospels, but it is the same Jesus whom it portrays.

A large amount of support for these seven themes is given by Paul's letters and by the Letter to the Hebrews. Considerable support comes also from the rest of the New Testament. The different writers are all witnesses to Jesus as the Christ. They have different styles of writing and different emphases, but they all point to one man. Their portraits of him are not identical, but they clearly depict the same person. With agreement of this nature, it is possible to speak of the biblical Jesus.

Much has been made of the differences between the accounts of Jesus in the New Testament. Matthew and Luke record his miraculous birth; the other writings do not. Some writings speak of his existence before his physical birth; others do not. Some give a more detailed account of his ethical teaching than others. Some elaborate the meaning of his death more than others. Some attach more importance to the future resurrection and judgement than do others; but these differences do not alter the basic consensus, which has been outlined.

The consensus is not affected by discrepancies in the chronological order of events in the gospels or by the precise wording of sayings. It is not even affected by an apparent variety of opinion as to whether the future resurrection of the dead will be physical or not. These are differences about details. There is agreement about the main themes. The consensus is not even affected by the expectation of some New Testament writers that the final event would come in the near future. Eager anticipation of the day when God's purpose will be completed is understandable. The important fact, however, is that the event was expected, whether it was to come soon or later.

All too often the differences between the New Testament writers have been allowed to obscure their clear agreement about the central themes. Their support for these themes makes it possible to speak of a biblical Jesus, who is not the subjective creation of individual interpreters but is recognizable as the one person to whom all the New Testament writers bear witness.

It may be asked whether it would be possible to supplement the biblical portraits of Jesus with impressions of him gleaned from other early Christian writings. In principle, of course, this is quite possible. The First Letter of Clement, the Didache and the Letters of Ignatius, were all written before AD 120, and it is possible that parts of the New Testament may have been written after them. They belong to the New Testament period, and in general they support the portraits of Jesus given in the Bible.

Problems arise, however, with the apocryphal gospels. These works are likely to have been written later than the New Testament. Some of them are preoccupied with spectacular and bizarre narratives of Jesus's infancy and boyhood, which make no serious contribution to any impression of him as saviour, revealer and teacher.[53] Others are devoted to the last days of his earthly life, and to some extent present a portrait of him similar to those contained in the Bible. One of them, however, the Gospel of Peter, differs sharply from the New Testament in that it implies that Jesus did not suffer pain on the cross and did not actually die before he was taken into heaven.[54] Another work, the Coptic Gospel of Thomas, consists entirely of sayings of Jesus, and does not give a narrative account of his activities. Some of these sayings, like the statement that every woman who becomes a man will enter the Kingdom of Heaven,[55] are hardly characteristic of the biblical Jesus. This gospel is notice-ably silent about the death of Jesus and his work of redemption. Its versions of some of his sayings imply that he reveals a secret knowl-edge to favoured individuals who will thereby be enabled to with-draw from the world into a spiritual realm. Although much of its teaching is in harmony with the biblical Jesus, in various respects it gives a Gnostic account of him. Other Gnostic writings, some of which bear the title of gospels, present impressions of Jesus which differ considerably from the biblical portraits of him.[56] In varying degrees they minimize the importance of his death, emphasize salva-tion by the acquisition of secret knowledge, and neglect the theme of a future climax to God's work of salvation. The earliest of these apocryphal gospels and other writings are dated to the second cen-tury. They are not as near to the events as most of the books of the New Testament. More important than the difference of date is the difference in quality of the portraits of Jesus. When we compare the biblical Jesus with these non-biblical impressions of him, we have to consider which Jesus makes the greater claim on us. Acceptance of the biblical Jesus in preference to the Jesus of these other writings is based on the strength of the claim exercised by the former. It pro-ceeds from a response to his intrinsic quality and power.

Acceptance of the Biblical Jesus

To accept the biblical Jesus is to accept the New Testament ac-counts of him as faithful impressions of his life and teaching. It is very easy to give only a partial acceptance to these impressions, by taking note of his actions but neglecting his teaching, or by giving recognition to his teaching but disregarding his actions. It is equally easy to give acceptance to only a limited selection of his activities, by disregarding, for example, the importance of his miracles. It is easy to give acceptance to only a limited selection of his teaching, to concentrate wholly on his words about himself or wholly on his words about daily conduct, or wholly on his words about the future. When the New Testament portraits of him are treated in this way, it is not the biblical Jesus, who is being accepted, but a disfigurement of him.

To accept the biblical Jesus is to yield to the power and authority of the Jesus of the New Testament writers. These portraits of him are the earliest that survive. No comparable surviving accounts of him were written as early as they were. Traditionally they have been regarded as the work of the apostles or their companions. Even if, as many scholars suggest, the traditions are not always correct, and some of the books were written by other authors, they took shape at a time when men and women who had known the earthly Jesus were still living. Most of the books were written during the first century AD. If they were not the work of eye witnesses, they were composed by writers, who had access to eye witnesses.

It is not their proximity to the events, however, which alone constitutes their claim to provide the definitive accounts of Jesus. It is the intrinsic quality of their portraits of him which plays the major part in constituting this claim. These portraits do not ask to be considered just as records of past events or as documents for the study of religions. They were composed in order to awaken or to confirm faith. They are themselves invitations to discipleship. The biblical Jesus awakens faith by his own power and persuasiveness.

The Christian interpreter of the Scriptures is the Jesus portrayed by the New Testament writers, not an arbitrary selection of certain features of him. Whatever views may be entertained about the sources and traditions used by the gospels, it is the New Testament writers themselves who are being trusted for conveying faithful impressions of him. It does not follow that they have given meticulously accurate accounts of every detail of the events of his life or a verbatim report of each of his sayings. Allowance has to be made for errors of detail, for lack of exactness about the dates and sequence of events, and for exaggeration and embellishment in the records of Jesus's sayings and actions. But acceptance of the biblical impressions of him means a recognition that he was the kind of man that the gospels depict him to be, who performed the kind of actions ascribed to him, including the miraculous. To begin with the assumption that he could not have performed miraculous actions is to set limits to the power of God. Acceptance of the biblical Jesus also means believing that he was crucified and really rose again. It means believing that he actually appeared to his disciples and communicated intelligibly with them after his resurrection.

To accept the biblical Jesus is also to accept the trustworthiness of the accounts of his teaching. They do not have the verbal accuracy of a tape-recorder. They were handed down orally for many years before they were put into writing, and they were translated from Aramaic into Greek, a procedure which would demand at least a measure of paraphrasing. It is more important, however, that they should give a faithful account of Jesus's message than that they should reproduce each saying with complete verbal exactness. For example, according to John's Gospel, Jesus said, 'Unless one is born anew, he cannot see the kingdom of God'.[57] Many scholars argue that Jesus could not have uttered these words because they reflect Hellenistic imagery and thought. This argument falls a long way short of being devastating. Galilee was on the fringe of the Hellenistic world, and Jesus is likely to have encountered Hellenistic ideas there. It is conceivable that he spoke about a new birth. But even if he did not utter the particular words ascribed to him, it is the consensus of the gospels that he promised new life to his followers. This is the meaning of his words about new birth. The essence of his message is more important than the precise words which he spoke.

Similar comments can be made about other sayings of Jesus. The basic issue is not whether Jesus pronounced the exact Aramaic equivalents of 'I am the light of the world', or 'I am the bread of life'.[58] It is whether he gave the impression by his teaching that he was uniquely related to God and uniquely the revealer of God, and that he could bring new life to men and women. 'I am' with its echo of the name of God in the Old Testament suggests a unique relationship to him. 'Light of the world' conveys the idea of divine revelation and guidance. 'Bread of life' implies that he is the giver of new life. These are the ideas which these sayings communicate. And acceptance of the biblical Jesus implies a reliance on the biblical accounts as trustworthy evidence about the essence of his message.

Acceptance of the biblical Jesus means acceptance of the main features of the biblical portraits of him, especially when a consensus of several witnesses can be discerned. This Jesus is not the subjective creation of modern writers. He clearly shines from the pages of the New Testament. Among the various functions which he performs is that of being the unique revealer of God. And one of the

ways in which he reveals God is by being the interpreter of the
Scriptures.

This acceptance is given to the earthly Jesus and not just to the
risen Christ. Indeed it is the earthly Jesus, who provides evidence
about the characteristics of the risen Christ. The New Testament
does not rely on private revelations received by early Christians to
give information about him. It relies on testimonies to his earthly
life. There are records of private revelations in the letters of Paul
and in the Book of Revelation. Paul says that he was once caught up
into Paradise, where he heard things that nobody may utter.[59] The
Book of Revelation tells of John's visions of the exalted Christ, but
the distinctive portrait of Jesus is found in the records of his earthly
life. The accounts of the resurrection affirm his victory over death
and contain statements about his gift of the Holy Spirit to his disciples and his continuing presence among them; but it is the accounts
of his earthly life, which provide the clearest and fullest information
about the way in which he behaved, about his attitude to people,
and about the teaching which he delivered. To recognize the importance of the testimonies to his earthly life does not imply a denial of
his resurrection. It implies the recognition that it is Jesus of Nazareth, not somebody else, who has risen from the dead. Towards the
end of the first century the belief arose in some parts of the Roman
Empire that Nero would return from the dead, a belief which influenced the descriptions of the Beast in the Book of Revelation. It
makes all the difference to the Christian message that it proclaims
the resurrection of Jesus and not of Nero. The information which
the New Testament provides about the earthly life of Jesus is essential, if we are to know what kind of man it was who rose from the
dead.

It is sometimes suggested that it does not matter whether Jesus
really performed the actions and uttered the sayings which are
ascribed to him in the gospels. It is argued that the gospels convey
the early Church's beliefs about the risen Christ, and that, if the
sayings of Jesus were not uttered during his earthly ministry, they
could still have been communicated by the exalted Christ to his
Church. This argument, however, contradicts the central theme of
the gospels, which is that God revealed himself and carried out his

work of salvation in an earthly life. It is integral to the biblical accounts of Jesus Christ that these actions and this teaching belong to a man who was subject to the conditions of human existence. If the emphasis is put wholly on the risen Jesus, the door is opened for a completely subjective account of him. Anyone can claim to have received visions of the risen Jesus, which may easily be treated as having equal weight with those in the Bible. Acceptance of the biblical portraits of Jesus means acceptance of the accounts of his earthly life as faithful records, which distinguish him from the leaders and prophets of Israel, and from the deities and heroes of other religions. It is this biblical Jesus, clearly portrayed in the New Testament, who is the distinctive Christian interpreter of the Scriptures.

5
The New Testament in the Light of Jesus

When the biblical Jesus acts as the interpreter of the Scriptures, all of their contents are to be seen in his light. He gives the stamp of his approval or disapproval to the views expressed in the Bible and to the conduct described there. No Christian account can be given of the Scriptures until they are placed under the scrutiny of Jesus himself. Whether attention is given to the whole of a book of the Bible or only to part of it, he is the criterion by which it is evaluated. If, under the influence of modern scholarship, consideration is given to the meaning of a saying or story at some conjectural earlier stage of its history, before it became part of the biblical book, Jesus is still the criterion. His function is vastly different from that of historical and literary criticism. When the Scriptures are read in his light, it is not their authorship, precise historical accuracy, literary form and structure which are being investigated, but the consistency of their teachings with Jesus himself.

The idea that the Scriptures should be judged at all may be unwelcome to people who regard them as the infallible words of God. If the Scriptures are inerrant, if they never make any mistake, they are not to be judged but only to be accepted. There can be no criterion, neither Jesus nor anyone else, by whom the sacred words can be assessed. In spite of a widespread tendency, however, to treat the Bible with a reverence which asks no questions about its authority or credibility, the very nature of the Scriptures makes it necessary to have a criterion by which to judge them. The Bible contains obvious inconsistencies. There is conflict about dates, the order of events, the wording of sayings, but the problem extends also to more important matters. The patterns of conduct which are commended in the Old Testament often conflict with that of Jesus. He himself speaks of the inadequacy of Old Testament teaching,[1] and Paul rejects the binding authority of the Jewish Law.[2] The presence of these disagreements makes it essential to have a standard of judgement if the Bible is to be used as Christian Scripture. It is Jesus, not the Bible itself, who is the basic authority for the Christian. Any authority which claims to be Christian, even the authority of the Bible, is derived from him, and therefore is subject to judgement by him. If the Bible is to be interpreted from a Christian viewpoint, it must be read in the light of Jesus.

The Gospels

The New Testament, as much as any other part of the Bible, is subject to the judgement of Jesus. All the sayings and stories in the gospels as well as all the contents of the Acts, Epistles, and Revelation have to be evaluated by him. It may seem strange that the gospels, which provide the main material for the biblical portraits of Jesus, should have to be judged by him. Yet even they need him as a criterion. Only too easily a distorted picture can be obtained of him by concentrating on a few stories and sayings at the expense of others. The whole Jesus and not part of him is the interpreter of the scriptures. His sayings and actions must not be seen in isolation from each other.

The danger of relying exclusively on a particular saying can be seen by examining Jesus's warning against anger. 'Every one who is angry with his brother', he said, 'shall be liable to judgment'.[3] If this saying alone is considered, the conclusion will be reached that Jesus was opposed to any kind of anger. But the gospel accounts of his behaviour portray him as a man who rebuked the demons and even rebuked Peter.[4] He was angry with the Pharisees who criticized him for healing a man on the Sabbath.[5] His strong denunciations of scribes and Pharisees as offspring of vipers, hypocrites, and whited sepulchres,[6] are evidence that he showed anger. He was angry too when he drove the moneychangers from the Temple.[7] His condemnation of anger in the Sermon on the Mount, therefore, must not be considered in isolation from his own example. An early copyist of the gospels inserted into the text of the Sermon on the Mount the explanation 'without cause' so that it read 'Everyone who is angry with his brother without cause shall be liable to judgment'.[8] The copyist's comment is a fair one. Jesus himself was angry in a righteous cause. He was angry when God was dishonoured by the abuse of the Temple and by the distortion of the Law. He was also angry when Peter tried to dissuade him from going to his death. He was not opposed to righteous indignation since he exhibited it himself. It is against petulant selfish anger that his teachings are directed. And those teachings must be understood in the light of the total portrait of Jesus.

The whole Jesus also interprets his sayings about violence. His instruction to turn the other cheek and refrain from resistance to evil might suggest, considered on its own, an attitude of complete passivity in the face of injustice. The saying needs to be read in conjunction with one of the most memorable incidents recorded in the gospels: the cleansing of the Temple.[9] Jesus took the initiative in driving the money changers out of the Temple. There was an element of aggressiveness in his action, although there is no evidence that he did physical violence to anybody. The story shows that Jesus cannot be written off as a man who refused to stand up for his beliefs, and the statements about non-violence in the Sermon on the Mount must be understood in conjunction with his own conduct. It would be a gross distortion of the facts, however, to conclude that he advocated the use of violence as a normal means of accomplishing his ends. One of the strongest emphases of the gospels is that he refused to be a violent revolutionary.[10] A particular saying or incident of the gospels has to be understood in the light of the whole Jesus.

The whole Jesus should also be used to understand particular sayings about his relationship to the law. In the Sermon on the Mount, he says that he came to fulfil the law and the prophets, not to abolish them.[11] This fulfilment cannot mean a complete obedience to every command of the law since in the very same Sermon on the Mount Jesus rejects the commandment 'an eye for an eye and a tooth for a tooth', and also disassociates himself from the Old Testament advocacy of the hatred of enemies.[12] Any interpretation of his

saying about fulfilment of the Law must recognize that in some respects he claimed to supersede the law. The idea of fulfilment must
be seen in terms of his fulfilment of the expectations of the Law and
the prophets, rather than of an acceptance of every detail of the
Law.[13]

In the above examples Jesus has been used as a criterion for the
understanding of his own sayings, which must be seen not in isolation but in relation to the total impression of him in the gospels.
Sometimes the whole Jesus can broaden the horizons of a saying by
showing new meanings, which are not apparent when it is read on
its own. For example, the saying, 'Blessed are the meek, for they
shall inherit the earth' acquires an enhanced importance when it is
recognized that in two other places in Matthew's Gospel Jesus himself is described as meek.[14] In the light of the whole Jesus, 'Blessed
are the meek' commends a quality, which is displayed by Jesus himself. When the whole Jesus is used as a key to understanding the
gospels, there will be no danger of using isolated verses or isolated
stories to formulate a distorted picture of him. Indeed other parts of
the gospels can be used to see deeper meanings in the material.

Paul's Letters

The use of Jesus as a criterion is essential for a Christian interpretation of Paul's letters. It is important not only to understand
what Paul intended to say but to decide how far he is authoritative
for Christians in the present day. The average modern reader is reluctant to accept all his teaching as authoritative, but suspects that
some of it may have been relevant only for past ages. If readers
merely accept the authority of those elements of Paul's teaching
which suit their own inclination, they use no authority but themselves. There is need for a criterion to decide whether Paul's words
are of permanent value or not. If his injunction that women should
have their heads covered while they are praying or prophesying is
no longer binding, should his prohibition of adultery continue to be
obligatory?[15] If it is no longer necessary to take seriously his ruling
that women should keep silent in church, is it important to accept
his exhortation to love one's neighbour?[16] If it is no longer appropriate to encourage slaves, as Paul did, to be obedient to their masters,

is there any need to take heed of his warning not to think more highly of oneself than one ought to think?[17] These and similar questions arise from a reading of Paul's letters. The answer to them is found in the biblical Jesus. He is the standard for deciding the relevance of Paul's message for today.

The rule that women should have their heads covered while they are praying or prophesying may have been important for the churches in first century Greece, when a woman with her head uncovered would be suspected of immorality. It is not, however, an essential requirement of the Christian life. When the biblical portraits of Jesus are examined, it can be seen that he made no rules about clothing. He was concerned with inner motives rather than outward appearance. Paul's instructions may have been suitable for the Corinthian church in his day but are not permanently binding. His instruction about the silence of women in church is another rule which belongs to a past age. It is hard to reconcile with Paul's recognition in the same letter that women may pray and prophesy.[18] This apparent contradiction may be explained by assuming that the women who prayed and prophesied were not doing so at formal worship, or that Paul was inconsistent. In any case there is no support from the biblical Jesus for the rule that women must keep silent in worship. Jesus did not speak about those matters. No doubt he was used to the practice of women remaining silent in the synagogue services, but he was unconcerned about legislating for matters of ritual. Moreover, his readiness to treat women on the same level socially as men suggests that he was not inclined to silence them. It is not that Jesus actually gave contrary instructions to those of Paul. His attitude indicates that Christianity does not stand or fall by regulations about these matters.

It is the same biblical Jesus who must be used as the criterion for Paul's teaching about slavery. The presence of instructions to slaves in Paul's writings was for a long time treated as a justification for the continuance of slavery. This was an unfair use of Paul, who never set the seal of his approval on the institution, and himself affirmed that in Christ there is neither slave nor free.[19] In case there should be any doubt about the Christian position, the last word does not rest with Paul but with the biblical Jesus, who showed a sympathy for the downtrodden members of society, which clashes sharply with any acceptance of the rightness of slavery.[20] It is not that Jesus passes judgement on the Pauline attitude, for there is uncertainty about Paul's position; but he does pass judgement on any interpretation of Paul, which would lead to the conclusion that slavery is acceptable.

While the use of the biblical Jesus as interpreter leads to the conclusion that certain injunctions of Paul are not permanently binding, it also leads to the conclusion that other teachings of his are relevant today. Paul's condemnation of sexual immorality, of adultery and fornication, has full support from the biblical Jesus.[21] His exhortations to love other people and to refrain from thinking too highly of oneself are in full accord with Jesus's teaching. At these and other points Paul has strong support from the biblical Jesus.[22] When Jesus is used as the criterion, the teaching is allowed to speak directly to us in our situation as well as to the inhabitants of the ancient world in theirs.

To look at Paul in the light of Jesus does not make Paul superfluous. It is not a question of rejecting out of hand any teaching that has no direct parallel in the gospels. The idea of the Church as the body of Christ,[23] which is not mentioned in the gospels, is thoroughly in harmony with the biblical Jesus, but introduces imagery and insights which are not present in the gospel portraits. The idea of life in Christ and the teaching about the gifts and fruit of the Spirit[24] both shed new light on the Christian message. They do not conflict with the biblical Jesus. They illuminate him. The same is true of Paul's teaching about justification by grace through faith.[25] This teaching is consistent with the Jesus of the gospels. In the parable of the Pharisee and the tax-collector Jesus says that the tax-collector who admitted his need of God's mercy went away justified rather than the self-righteous Pharisee, who boasted of his own spiritual achievements.[26] Jesus's call to 'repent and believe in the gospel', and his readiness to forgive sinners are evidence of God's initiative in seeking the sinners and offering them forgiveness;[27] all of this is in agreement with the doctrine of justification, with its emphasis on God's willingness to give acceptance to those people who put their trust in him. John's Gospel teaches that grace has come through Jesus Christ, and that those who believe in him receive eternal life;[28]

this is consistent with the teaching of Paul, but Paul with his incisive way of stating and developing the doctrine has a special contribution to make.

When Paul's letters are read in the light of Jesus, most of their contents are seen to be in harmony with him. Paul's teaching about the mercy, grace and love of God, his expectations about the future, his liberal attitude to ritual, and his high ethical standards are in basic accord with the example and teaching of Jesus as portrayed in the gospels.

The Letter of James

One of the New Testament letters which has often received adverse criticism is the Letter of James. By contrast with Paul, who teaches justification by faith apart from works of law, James says that works as well as faith are needed for justification.[29] This difference may be partly explained by the fact that James's notion of faith is confined to the acceptance of doctrines and lacks the richness of Paul's understanding of faith as complete trust in Christ. There are, however, other matters for which the letter has been criticized. It mentions Jesus by name only twice, says nothing about his crucifixion, or his earthly life, and contains only limited reference to the grace of God;[30] but it is not an essential requirement that a letter as short as this should contain a full and rounded statement of the gospel, and in fact, the letter includes a considerable amount of material which is in harmony with the teaching of Jesus. Some parts of it are reminiscent of his very words, his warnings about riches and about judging others, his sayings about the swearing of oaths.[31] The law of love is central for James as for Jesus.[32] Even the letter's emphasis on the need for works has a parallel in the words of Jesus,[33] but James is not just an echo of the gospels. His teaching about the problems created by the presence of wealthy persons in the Church and his instructions to teachers[34] provide insights which are not found in the gospels but are thoroughly consistent with the outlook of Jesus.

The Book of Revelation

Jesus acts as criterion for all the New Testament writings, but apart from the gospels, Paul and James, attention will here be confined to the Book of Revelation. Some students of this work see it chiefly as a repository of clues to the course of future history. With its aid they predict the date of the return of Christ to earth and the nature of the events preceding it. But the biblical Jesus does not expect his followers to know the map of the future in detail. 'Take heed', he says, 'watch; for you do not know when the time will come'. And after his resurrection he tells them, 'It is not for you to know times or seasons which the Father has fixed by his own authority'. He himself pleads ignorance of these matters: 'But of that day,' he says, 'or that hour no one knows, not even the angels in heaven, nor the Son, but only the Father'.[35] Human curiosity has led many inquirers to speculate about the future, and often they have concluded that Jesus Christ was shortly to return to earth, only to be proved mistaken by subsequent events. Undoubtedly the Book of Revelation is concerned to make predictions about the future, but if it is read with Jesus as its interpreter, attention will be paid mainly to other aspects of its message. It was written in a time of persecution, to encourage its readers to remain faithful to Christ, even when they were ordered to worship the emperor. Its warnings and encouragements have great relevance for daily life in every age. The mysterious Beast, to which it frequently refers, [36] clearly represents either a human ruler or a human government that is claiming to be divine. It is more important to pay heed to the book's powerful warnings about the danger of worshipping human institutions and authorities than to speculate about the precise identity of the Beast. To respond to its exhortations to faithfulness is more important than to use it as a time chart of future events.

Problems arise about the accounts of eternal torment in the Book of Revelation. It is certainly consistent with the portraits of Jesus in the rest of the New Testament that warnings of judgement should be uttered. The pictures of eternal punishment in the Book of Revelation, however, display a ferocity which exceeds anything in the rest of the New Testament.[37] Moreover, plagues, earthquakes and other forms of destruction are predicted as punishments to be sent on earth by God and his angels.[38] When these prophecies are interpreted as Christian Scripture, they must be examined in the light of the total impression of the biblical Jesus.

Of course, the Book of Revelation itself provides some of the evidence about the biblical Jesus. It is the risen Christ, the heavenly Lamb, who is said to introduce the visions,[39] but these visions need to be seen in the light of the biblical Jesus as a whole. An all-important question is whether they are consistent with the teaching and example of the earthly Jesus. If they are taken as exact literal predictions about God's behaviour in the future, they are not all in accord with the other biblical impressions of Jesus, but if they are treated as poetic expressions of a belief in God's ultimate triumph and as vivid warnings of the danger of being totally and finally alienated from God, they are in harmony with the other portraits of Jesus in the New Testament.

The Book of Revelation is a majestic and imposing work. In times of cruel persecution its author affirmed his undiminished confidence in the power and justice of God. Its exhortations to faithfulness and its assurances of God's ultimate victory are in harmony with the Jesus of the rest of the New Testament. It is for these aspects of its message that it is most to be prized.

In the above discussions of New Testament writings special attention has been paid to passages where there appear to be inconsistencies in the accounts of the teaching and example of Jesus, or where there seems to be a conflict between the teaching of a New Testament writer and the biblical impressions of Jesus. Most of the New Testament, however, is fully in harmony with his example and message. The teachings of its writers are for the most part in accord with his teachings. They speak of the dependence of men and women on God, and God's love for them. They tell of God's work of salvation in Jesus Christ, and look forward with confidence to God's ultimate triumph. They commend the virtues of love, mercy, kindness, gentleness, humility, sexual purity, freedom from love of money, and avoidance of violence. The New Testament, which includes the definitive portraits of Jesus, is with few exceptions in harmony with him.

6
The Old Testament in the Light of Jesus

When the Old Testament is read in the light of Jesus, much of it falls below his standard. The great heroes of the Hebrew tradition were men with feet of clay. Noah was found drunk in his tent. Abraham was prepared to let his wife sleep with Pharaoh in order to save his own life. Jacob deceived his father in order to obtain privileges which ought to have belonged to his brother. David is notorious for his affair with Bathsheba.[1]

If it was only the conduct of these heroes which was contrary to the standards of Jesus, there would be no problem about the Old Testament's inspiration and authority. It would be sufficient to recognize that these men displayed in ample measure the human condition of sinfulness. Greater difficulty arises over passages in the Old Testament where the teaching about God seems to conflict with the standards of Jesus. The story of the flood, for example, describes how God, having repented of the creation of the human race, decided to exterminate it with the exception of Noah and his family. There seems to be no mercy in such a decision. According to the Book of Exodus, God destroyed all the firstborn of the Egyptians, although these unfortunate persons do not appear to have been any worse that the rest of their nation, who survived them. Frequently it is asserted that God raised up foreign conquerors to punish Israel by making war on them, sacking their cities, and slaughtering or enslaving their inhabitants.[2] This picture of God does not harmonize with the standards of love and justice advocated by Jesus. An attempt is sometimes made to remove the offensiveness of this portrait by explaining that God did not actually cause these catastrophes but merely allowed them to happen. The fact remains, however, that the Old Testament unequivocally asserts that God brought about these disasters.

God is also said to have instructed the Israelites to perpetrate wholesale massacres in time of war. According to the Jewish Law, God required the Israelite army to slaughter all the adult males in any non-Palestinian city which was captured after resistance. All the women and children were to be taken into captivity. Harsher treatment was provided for Palestinian cities which resisted. Every human being and every animal in them were to be put to death without respect to age or sex. It was this kind of treatment, which was meted out by Joshua to the inhabitants of Jericho. All of them were massacred, with the exception of the household of the prostitute Rahab, who had given assistance to Israelite spies on a previous occasion. The same treatment was later extended to the Amalekites. At God's command, Samuel ordered Saul to massacre all their men, women, children and animals. When Saul spared their king Agag together with some of their livestock, Samuel completed the unfinished task by hewing Agag in pieces. Another memorable story concerns the Midianites. At God's bidding, Moses is said to have ordered the slaughter of all their males together with all the women who were not virgins, and to have handed over the virgins to the Israelite men.[3] Psalm 137 is fully in harmony with the moral outlook of these stories. It begins with a beautiful lament by the Jewish exiles in Babylon, but ends with a vicious blessing on anyone who succeeds in murdering the infant children of the Babylonians. This psalm is only one of several imprecatory psalms which display a similar vindictiveness.[4] These psalms, like the stories of massacres which have been mentioned, have a far different morality from that of the biblical Jesus.

In spite of the approval which is given by some of its writings to these sentiments and actions, the Old Testament is regarded as Scripture by Christians. Indeed it was the only Scripture which the first generation of Christians possessed. It is indispensable for an understanding of Christianity, since neither the New Testament nor the early Church can be adequately studied without it. Moreover, its books have a power and a message of their own, which would merit

serious consideration, even if they were not regarded as Scripture;
but when they are given a Christian interpretation, they must be
read in the light of Jesus Christ and judged by his standards.

One of the most common errors of popular Christianity is its
treatment of the Old Testament as equally authoritative with Jesus.
The Old Testament can be used to justify actions which are completely contrary to his way. Bloodthirsty massacres can be perpe-
trated with appeals to it. Stern and remorseless justice can be practised on the basis of the Jewish Law, without regard to Jesus's own
rejection of the principle of retribution and without regard to his
advocacy of mercy. If the Scriptures are to be understood from a
Christian standpoint, they must be seen not from Mount Sinai,
where Moses received the law, but from Calvary, where Jesus died.

A Christian interpretation of the Old Testament is not the same
as a Jewish interpretation of it. However instructive and illuminat-
ing may be the interpretations of it given from the point of view of
Judaism, they did not see it from the standpoint of Jesus. Nor is a
Christian interpretation the same as the attempt of a scholar to understand the Scriptures from the viewpoint of the biblical authors
and their sources. Nor is it the same as the endeavour of some literary critics to unfold the meaning of a text by considering the structure of the text itself. Christian interpretation has a distinctive concern, which marks it off from other kinds of interpretation. It
proceeds from the acceptance of Jesus as the Christ; and it seeks to
understand the Old Testament in the light of Jesus.

When a Christian interpretation is sought for Old Testament
passages, which appear to be in conflict with the standards of Jesus,
there are three approaches which can be used. One is to take the
passage at its face value and treat it as a faithful account of God's
will. This approach, exemplified by the fifth century commentator
Theodoret, leads to the conclusion that the destruction of Jericho
was a demonstration of God's power, and that it was right to massacre some of the Midianite women, because, if they had been spared,
they would have corrupted their captors with false doctrines. The
same commentator argues that Samuel killed Agag because it was
his pious duty to obey God's command and that the Psalmist was
justified in advocating the murder of Babylonian babies, because

the Babylonians had treated the Jewish children with equal cruelty.[5] This approach disregards the example and teaching of Jesus. By his standards the violence and cruelty, with which the Israelites treated the Midianite women, was totally reprehensible. In his teaching the principle of retribution, by which Theodoret excused the Psalmist's attitude to the Babylonian infants, was explicitly rejected.[6]

A second approach to these passages is to give them a spiritual interpretation. An example of this is to be found in the third century theologian Origen's homilies on the Book of Joshua. Origen sees in the book's account of the battle of Jericho a symbolic reference to Jesus's triumph over the world. Jericho stands for this world, and the destruction of Jericho for the end of this age. Origen also argues that the Midianites who were destroyed at the command of Moses symbolize the vices of human flesh which can be overcome by prayer, fasting and a virtuous life.[7] The same approach is found in the eighth-century scholar Bede's treatment of the story of Samuel and Agag.[8] Bede argues that Agag stands for pride in the human soul, which we must eradicate. A further example of this kind of interpretation is Augustine's treatment of Psalm 137, where the Babylonian infants are said to stand for the evil desires which are born in the corrupt human soul.[9] Augustine, who lived in the late fourth and early fifth centuries, advises his readers to eradicate these desires while they are still small, and before they have acquired strength. These writers do not actually deny that the massacres recorded in the Old Testament were committed or that the Psalmist encouraged the murder of the Babylonian babies. But they focus on the spiritual meaning as the truly important meaning for Christian readers.

A third approach is to give full recognition to the literal meaning, but to recognize that it is not in harmony with the biblical Jesus. Such is the way of the fourth-century theologian and preacher, John Chrysostom in his comments on Psalm 137. He says that the feelings expressed are not those of the Psalmist but those of the Jews, and that they do not agree with the teaching of the New Testament. 'Whenever', he writes, 'he describes the feelings of others, he depicts their anger, their pain; which indeed he has done even now, bringing out the passion of the Jews who extended their wrath even to the generation of infants. But such is not the teaching of the New Testament. We are commanded to give our enemies drink and food, to pray for those who despitefully use us'.[10] Chrysostom is using Jesus as the criterion and is prepared to admit that the sentiments of this psalm fall below Jesus's standard.[11]

Of these three approaches the first is inadequate because it accepts standards other than those of Jesus. The second is worth consideration, but only after the third approach has been taken. It is this third kind of interpretation, which is basic. If a passage is being examined, it is of primary importance to discover its literal meaning and decide if its intention is in harmony with the standard of Jesus. Then it must be asked if it gives special insight into issues connected with the Christian message and the Christian life. At this stage the so-called spiritual meaning may be investigated, but conflict of the literal meaning with the standards of Jesus cannot be overlooked.

Examples have been given of stories and sayings, which are likely to come under adverse judgement from Jesus, but there is plenty of other material which is thoroughly in harmony with him. Affirmations in the psalms about God's bounty in creation, his mercy to the penitent sinner, and his love of righteousness are fully in agreement with the teaching and example of Jesus. The passionate concern of the prophets for justice, their fearlessness in denouncing injustice, their concern for purity of motive, and their hostility to a merely formal and outward piety are completely in accord with him. The firm trust in God and loyalty to him shown by patriarchs and prophets and other heroes in time of crisis are characteristic of the way of life which Jesus advocates: Abraham's readiness to go out into the unknown in order to reach the promised land, Moses's determined courage in the face of Pharaoh, Nathan's fearless denunciation of David, Elijah's faith and endurance under persecution by Ahab and Jezebel, and Jeremiah's patience and persistence under oppression,[12] are fully consistent with the standards commended by Jesus. The use of Jesus as a criterion does not result in a devaluation of the Old Testament.

Indeed the Old Testament illuminates the understanding of the biblical Jesus. The whole world of the New Testament is unintelligible without it. The idea of the Messiah, the use of the titles 'Son of God' and 'Lord', the concepts of righteousness and love and of mercy and law, and the idea of the divine providence have their origins in the Jewish Scriptures. Many of the statements about Jesus in the New Testament contain Old Testament allusions, without which the meaning cannot be grasped. While the biblical Jesus acts as the criterion of the Old Testament, the reader's ability to understand him is in turn enhanced by a study of its contents.

Moreover, whereas the New Testament is the product of an oppressed minority group within the Roman Empire, the Old Testament is the book of a whole nation. Hence the Old Testament deals more fully than the New Testament with the responses of different areas of society to the claims of God. It shows the messengers of God in direct encounter with rulers more frequently and in more detail than does the New Testament. The duties and responsibilities of governors and rulers are faced more fully in the Old Testament than in the New Testament. Yet a Christian answer cannot be given to these issues apart from the biblical Jesus.

As the criterion, Jesus passes judgement on both the Old and the New Testaments. He decides whether actions and words and statements by the writers are in harmony with him or in conflict with him. Only when the Scriptures are in accord with him, do they speak with authority for the Christian. Indeed such authority as they possess is derived from the biblical Jesus, who is himself the ultimate authority. The Bible is the territory from which the gold is mined, but he is the touchstone for estimating the value of the material which the Bible provides. To accept him as the criterion is not to undervalue the biblical writers. It is to recognize that, however much God revealed himself through these writers, Jesus Christ is God's supreme revelation of himself.

The Authority of the Biblical Jesus

The biblical Jesus, not the whole Bible, is the authority for Christians. There has been much discussion about both the authority of the Bible and that of the Church. One viewpoint is that the Bible has authority only because it has been authorized as Scripture by the Church. Another viewpoint is that the Church can only exercise its authority legitimately, when it submits to the authority of the Scriptures. The basic authority, however, is neither that of the Bible nor that of the Church. It is that of the biblical Jesus. His authority does not depend on his presence within the collection of books called the Bible any more than on the approval of church councils. It exists in its own right, exercising its claims because of its own intrinsic merits.

In the early Church there was disagreement about which books were to be included in the New Testament. Although by AD 200 most of its present contents were generally accepted by the Church as Scripture, there was dispute about the status of Hebrews, James, 2 Peter, 2 and 3 John, Jude and Revelation. Eventually pronouncements were made, first by Athanasius, bishop of Alexandria, in 367, then by the Synod of Carthage in 397, declaring that the twenty-seven books now known as the New Testament were Christian Scripture. Church leaders were responsible for the decision that these disputed books should be included and that certain other books, to which consideration had been given, should be excluded. Since Jesus himself, rather than the Bible, is the authority, it is not of supreme importance that the collection should contain these disputed books and none of the rejected ones. If the Church had included in the New Testament the Letter of Barnabas, which it rejected, instead of the Letter of Jude, which it accepted, there would have been little difference, if any, in the impression made by the biblical Jesus today. It is from the four gospels and from the letters of Paul that the main impressions of him come; and these writings were accepted as Scripture by the end of the second century. The main sources for a knowledge of the biblical Jesus had established themselves as Scripture at an early date, not through the decree of a church council, or any other known church authority. Church councils had to make a decision about the disputed books, and the portraits of Jesus in those books, especially in Hebrews, are of great value; but Christianity does not stand or fall by them. The biblical Jesus had already made his impact and obtained recognition before a decision was made about the writings over which the Church showed hesitation. Church councils determined the limits of the New Testament, but the authority of the biblical Jesus exists independently of their decisions.

There was disagreement also about the precise limits of the Old Testament, a disagreement which persists to the present day. Protestants accept as the Old Testament the books which are contained in the Hebrew Bible. Roman Catholics also accept a number of additional books, which are in the Greek version of the Jewish Bible and are placed by Protestants in the collection known as the Old Testament Apocrypha. Because the basic authority is Jesus, it is not a matter of primary importance whether the Catholic or the Protestant verdict on the limits of the Old Testament should be accepted. In Jesus's own day the Jews themselves had not agreed about the Canon of their Scriptures. There was controversy about some of the books in the Greek version of their Bible and also about Esther, Ecclesiastes and the Song of Solomon. If Jesus and the first Christians could have a sure faith at a time when the limits of the Scriptures were undetermined, modern Christians can also maintain their faith at a time when there is disagreement between Catholics and Protestants about the limits of the Old Testament. Difference of opinion about this matter does not affect either the impact or the authority of the biblical Jesus.

The Bible is the Church's sacred book. It is the common heritage of Christians. The Church needs the Bible. Without the Bible the Church would not have the collection of writings which contain its enduring message, and which contain the evidence for its basic authority, the biblical Jesus. The Bible needs the Church. Without the Church the Bible would have no community within which its message could be interpreted. But both Bible and Church depend on the biblical Jesus to validate their claim to be Christian. It is not a question of the Bible's dependence on the Church or the Church's dependence on the Bible. They both obtain their credentials from the biblical Jesus. When the Church submits to him, it lives up to its name of Christian. When the Bible is interpreted by him, it can function as Christian Scripture. He is the authority. They are subordinate to him.

The Church's traditions are no more the ultimate authority than is the Church itself. They too depend on the biblical Jesus to authenticate their claim to be Christian. The practices and teachings of the Church may often deal with issues that were not explicitly faced by Jesus. As attempts to understand and carry out the will of God in various areas of human life, these traditions have to be taken seriously, but their authority depends on the extent to which they are in harmony with Jesus.

The same is true of the claim of individuals to have an authority within themselves, whether they describe it as reason or as the Holy Spirit. It is important to use human reason to reflect on issues of conduct and belief. It can point out logical inconsistencies in any teaching which is being considered. It can point out the implications of Jesus's message and the probable consequences of living in obedience to him. It can suggest methods of discussing the Scriptures. It can recognize the appropriateness of certain truths about conduct. It can suggest new ideas, especially in matters about which no clear guidance is given by Jesus. But it is not the ultimate authority. Since the whole self accepts Jesus as the authority, reason participates in that response of acceptance. Once it has recognized him as the Lord, reason is the servant, and he is the master.

Inward authority is also spoken of in terms of the indwelling presence of the Holy Spirit. People say that by the impulse of the Spirit they receive instruction about their actions in daily life. They believe that the Spirit brings truths to mind which were not uttered by Jesus in the New Testament. Yet so conflicting are the claims which have been made about the Spirit's guidance, that a standard is needed to test the genuineness of these claims. To make sure that the thoughts which come into our minds are not from 'a lying spirit' but from the Holy Spirit, we must turn to the biblical Jesus, and examine whether the thoughts are in harmony with him. The Spirit is the Spirit of Christ. There is no essential difference between 'Christ in us' and 'the Holy Spirit in us'. It is not that the Spirit's authority is subordinate to that of the biblical Jesus; the two are in complete accord with each other. The biblical Jesus is to be used to test the genuineness of any claim to inward divine guidance.

People assert that God's will can be found in the Scriptures, in the Church and its traditions, in the judgements of human reason and through inspiration of the Spirit. But these claims need always to be tested by the criterion of the impression of Jesus which can be discerned in the Bible. The biblical Jesus is the sure criterion of what is in accordance with the divine will. He is the ultimate authority. The Church, human reason and spiritual experience, just as much as Old and New Testaments, are to be seen in his light.

The authority of the biblical Jesus is also independent of the identity of the authors of the New Testament books. Traditionally these writings have been regarded as the work of apostles or their companions; and this connexion with the apostles was an important factor in their admission to the Bible. Serious questions have been raised about the authorship of many of the writings, but even if some of them may not be the work of the authors to whom they are ascribed, they are likely to have been written by disciples of apostles. The authority of the biblical Jesus, however, does not depend on the authorship of the writings in which he is portrayed. It depends on the quality of the portraits themselves. It is important that the books were written early, most, if not all, of them within a century of his death and resurrection. Their proximity to the events strengthens the claim of their portraits of him to consideration, but the authority of the biblical Jesus resides in his own intrinsic merit and power.

7
Letting the New Testament Speak for Today

When Jesus interprets the Bible, he provides a means by which it can give challenge, assurance, warning and instruction to men and women. He draws out its relevance for the present day. When the meaning of a passage in its original setting has been recognized to be in harmony or discord with the biblical Jesus, further questions have still to be asked in order to find out its importance for today. These questions are about our encounter with Jesus as we read or hear the Scriptures. They are about the ways in which we find him there. They are also about the ways in which we find God, ourselves and other people in the very places where we discover Jesus.

Often in discussions of the Scriptures people talk about identifying themselves with someone in the story which is being told. They claim that when they identify themselves with that person, the Scriptures come to life for them. The word 'identify' is not, however, wholly adequate for this purpose. Not always is the identification complete. For a short time a student of the Scriptures may experience the emotion of actually being present in the event described, but on reflection the reaction changes. It is not a matter of complete identification. We find similarities between ourselves and the people described in the Bible, but we also find contrasts. We do not actually participate in the event, but we see a likeness between our situation and theirs. If we think about the experience, we cease to have the feeling of being present there. In many cases it is a matter of similarity and contrast, not of identity. We can, however, always expect to discover ourselves in the study of the Scriptures, even though we do not actually identify ourselves with any of the men and women mentioned there. Instead, therefore, of using the term 'identification' it is more appropriate to speak of 'discovery'. Sometimes we may actually identify ourselves with people in the Scriptures, but this is not always the case. Sometimes we may be struck by the similarity or contrast between ourselves and the characters in a Bible narrative. Yet whether it is a case of identity or similarity or contrast, there can always be a point of discovery for the self.

It is not only in relation to the self that the term 'discovery' is preferable to 'identification'. When Jesus himself is found in the reading of a passage of Scripture he may not be actually mentioned in the words themselves, but there may be similarity or contrast between him and one of the persons mentioned in the Scripture. Thus, even when he is not directly to be found in the Scripture, he may be discovered in the reading of it by noticing the similarity or contrast between him and that person. The same observation is true of the discovery of the self in the Bible, and also the discovery of other people. They may be explicitly present there, or they may be discovered through similarities and contrasts.

To give a Christian interpretation of a biblical passage it is important to recognize the places where Jesus, God, the self, and other people can be found. These are the strategic points from which the passage can be seen to be relevant for the present day, even though it may have originally been intended for a situation in the ancient world. When we establish the places where these discoveries can be made, Jesus himself will address us through the Scriptures. Their words of challenge and encouragement, of warning and of promise can be received in our world and related to our lives. In these places where Jesus, God, the self and others are discovered, Jesus illuminates the Scriptures and lets his light shine on those who read or hear them.

Discovering Jesus

Jesus himself is easy to discover in the New Testament. All its writings bear witness to him. Gospels, Acts, Epistles and the Book of Revelation, although they are different forms of literature, agree in proclaiming him as the Lord and the Christ. He is the man who calls disciples, utters teaching, heals the sick, forgives sinners, was crucified and raised from the dead. His place in these narratives is beyond dispute. He is discovered there by his *presence*. In sayings also, as well as narratives, his presence can be seen. When he speaks of the Son of God and the Son of man, he is speaking of himself. When he predicts his suffering and death, his resurrection and his return to earth at the last day, and when he makes pronouncements about his relationship to God, he is present in the very saying itself. In words as well as in deeds Jesus himself is there.

In other passages he is discovered by his *similarity* to one of the people mentioned. The parables provide good examples of this aspect of discovery. He is like the son for whom a king makes a marriage feast, the nobleman who goes into a far country and returns to receive an account from his servants, and a farmer who sows good seed in his ground.[1] There are scholars who would quarrel with these explanations on the ground that a parable in its pure form contains no element of allegory. They would argue that the parables do not intend to liken Jesus to a king's son, or a nobleman, or a farmer.[2] It has not been proved, however, that Jesus could not have used allegory. Since allegory was not unknown in his world, he could well have made use of it himself.[3] Moreover, the writers of the gospels regarded these parables allegorically, and saw similarities to Jesus in the characters described there. Since the Jesus who is being sought is the Jesus of the biblical writers, it is legitimate to discover him where the writers intended him to be found.

Jesus may also be discovered by his similarity to symbols in the Book of Revelation. He is likened to a rider on a white horse. He is depicted as a lion and as a lamb.[4] He does not have all the characteristics of the animals to which he is likened, but shares some of them: the courage of the lion and the meekness of the lamb. The poetic imagery conveys truth about him which enables him to be encountered in these passages.

Where there is similarity, there is also *contrast*. He is like a nobleman, but does not have a large estate or material wealth. He is like a farmer, but does not look after his ground in the literal sense. He is like a lion or a lamb, but, being a man, he is different from them. Similarity and contrast accompany each other.

Jesus can also be the *authority* behind biblical teaching, as Paul recognizes when he makes a distinction between advice which he himself gives, and commands which were specifically given by the Lord.[5] He indicates that Jesus's words have a higher authority than his own. The gospels themselves attach importance to Jesus's teaching. He taught with authority and not as the scribes. The very words which he utters are Spirit and life.[6] Even though a saying of his contains no explicit statement about himself, it is his saying; he is to be discovered there as the authority who utters it.

Discovering God

God, as well as Jesus, is to be found in the New Testament. There are few passages where he is not explicitly mentioned. But he is not only to be found where he is specifically named. A Christian interpretation discovers him wherever Jesus is to be found. 'No one has ever seen God', says John's Gospel, 'the only Son, who is in the bosom of the Father, he has made him known',[7] and in Matthew's Gospel, Jesus says: 'No one knows the Father except the Son and any one to whom the Son chooses to reveal him'.[8] God's presence can be discerned in Jesus's statements about his authority to forgive sins, his Lordship of the Sabbath, his coming again as judge, and his raising of the dead at the last day.[9] It occurs in a more allusive way after he has stilled the storm when the disciples say, 'Who then is this that even the wind and sea obey him?', words which are reminiscent of statements made about God in the Psalms.[10]

God is to be found in the same place as Jesus in statements about Christ's activity in the creation of the world. According to Colossians and Hebrews, the world was made through Christ,[11] and according to John's Gospel, Jesus is the incarnation of the Word that was active in the creation.[12] Although the full implications of these assertions is not easy to decide, they clearly presuppose a doctrine of the incarnation. The Word of God was made flesh as Jesus of Nazareth. The God who was responsible for the creation of the world was incarnate in him.

God is also to be found in the passages which refer to the activity of the Holy Spirit. In the Bible the Spirit is God in action in human beings and in the rest of the universe. At Pentecost God was present when the disciples were filled with the Spirit.[13] When Paul says that the Spirit of God dwells in him,[14] that very statement is a place where God can be discovered. When Jesus says that the Spirit will lead his disciples into all truth,[15] that very saying is a discovery-point for God.

In most passages of the New Testament God is discovered by his *presence*. When he is named as God, he is clearly there. When Jesus is named, he is present in Jesus. He is there when the Spirit is said to be in action. Theologians may debate about the precise nature of that presence. Indeed that has been the theme of much controversy in the history of Christian thought. Debate about the correct ac- count of Christ's divinity and humanity and about the relationship between Father, Son and Spirit has engaged the minds of theolo- gians from the early days of the Church's life. But if serious atten- tion is paid to the biblical accounts, there is no doubt that God is regarded as present in Jesus and present in the Spirit.

It is possible also to find God in passages of the New Testament by *similarity*. Such is the case in some of the parables, at any rate in so far as they are treated allegorically. God is like a king, who made a marriage feast for his son.[16] God is like a man, who let his vine- yard out to tenants and sent his son to obtain some of the fruit;[17] but this similarity is accompanied by *contrast*. God is like a king but is not the same as an earthly king. God is like an owner of a vine- yard but is different from a human landowner. Yet usually in the New Testament God is to be discovered not by similarity and con- trast but by presence.

Discovering Ourselves

The books of the Bible are all intended to convey a message which directly impinges on the lives of the readers. They are not concerned merely to supply information about past events or about other people's points of view. Their intent is to speak to the readers in their situation; not only do they have a highly important message for their original readers, but their relevance also extends to every- one who reads or hears them. The Bible is never just about someone else.

Readers may sometimes identify themselves completely with the person addressed in the New Testament. They may discover them-

selves in the pages of the Scriptures by their *presence*. Commandments of universal scope apply directly to men and women in every
age. 'You shall love the Lord your God' and 'You shall love your
neighbour as yourself'[18] do not refer merely to Jews and Christians
of the first century. Everyone is included in the 'You'. There is also
the same universal relevance in Jesus's warnings about the danger of
riches, in his teaching on marriage and divorce, and in his exhortations to repentance and humility. The gospel writers did not assume
that his challenge was limited to a few groups of people. The authors of the Epistles and the Book of Revelation also contain much
teaching which has universal validity. The commend a way of life
which is recognizably the same as that which was advocated by
Jesus. Readers of the New Testament should expect to be themselves challenged and encouraged by what they encounter in its
pages. They should be willing to discover themselves in the persons
for whom the writings were originally intended.

The self can also be discovered by *similarity* to characters in the
biblical passages. Individuals may see their own conduct to be
comparable to Peter's in his denial of Jesus or to the rich young
ruler's in his refusal to sell his property.[19] They may liken themselves to Mary when she sat listening to the words of Jesus, or to the
disciples when Jesus washed their feet.[20] In the parable of the Rich
Fool, who died at the moment of his greatest prosperity, they may
see a warning to themselves.[21] In the parable of the Widow, whose
persistent pleas were answered by the judge, they may find assurance that their own prayers may be answered by God.[22]

When Paul tells the Christians at Corinth how to deal with the
problems of their church, he is directly addressing the Christians at
Corinth in the first century AD.[23] But the position of modern readers
is similar to that of those early Christians. In the modern world, as
in the ancient world, people are tempted on every side to be immoral; the very existence of the institution of marriage is threatened, the
Church is divided, and worship is often tawdry and insincere. Paul
can challenge modern Christians as he challenged the Christians at
Corinth. When they recognize the similarity of their situation to
that of the Corinthians, they can respond to the message of Paul's
letters.

Readers of the New Testament can also discover themselves there by *contrast*. They can perceive the difference between themselves and the people mentioned in the Scriptures. They can recognize that they lack the faith of the centurion who trusted in Jesus's ability to heal his servant.[24] They can admit that they do not share the love and adoration for Jesus displayed by the woman who anointed him.[25] They may find themselves to be unprepared for Christ, by contrast with the bridesmaids whose lamps were trimmed.[26] They may not be ready to sacrifice everything for God's Kingdom, by contrast with the readiness of the merchant to sell all his possessions for the pearl of great price.[27] They may lack the faith, courage and boldness displayed by the Christians whose deeds are recorded in the Acts of the Apostles.[28]

They may also find a contrast between themselves and a person who is to be viewed in a negative light. They may be unlike the man who buried his talent in the ground and failed to use it for the benefit of his master,[29] but since the books of the Bible are not primarily concerned to promote complacency, this type of contrast should be practised with caution. It is more conducive to self-flattery than to self-criticism. Contrasting interpretation is more effectively employed to create an awareness of one's deficiencies than of one's virtues.

Sometimes individuals do not encounter a definite similarity or contrast with themselves in the Scripture, but face a challenge to decision between two alternative ways of life. Will they be like the man who buried his talent in the ground, or those who invested their talents and profited from them? Will they be like the bridesmaids who were prepared or those who were unprepared for the bridegroom's arrival? Will they or will they not resemble Peter in his readiness to preach boldly in the face of persecution?[30] Will they or will they not, like the rich young ruler, refuse to give everything away for Christ?[31]

People may discover themselves in a *group* as well as in individuals. Many passages challenge the reader as a member of the Church, the people of God. The words, 'Fear not, little flock, for it is your Father's good pleasure to give you the kingdom',[32] were addressed first to the original disciples, but continue to give encouragement to

subsequent generations of his followers. When Paul described the
Church as the body of Christ,[33] he meant the Church in every time
and place, not just the Christian community in Corinth or Rome.
When Peter called the Christian people a royal priesthood,[34] he was
not only concerned with the communities in Asia Minor, to which
his letter was addressed, but with all Christ's people. The same possibilities of discovery are available for the Church as for the individual. It may be discovered by its actual *presence* in the Scripture
when the universal Church is spoken of. Or it may be discovered by
its *similarity* to a Christian community in the New Testament. Its
behaviour may resemble behaviour of the early Church in Corinth
or Rome or Galatia or Jerusalem. It may indeed sometimes be
closer in its outlook to non-Christian groups in the ancient world
than to the Church. It may recall the Pharisees with their legalism or
the Sadducees with their worldly aims and methods and unbelief
about the future; or it may be like the people at Athens described in
the Acts, who spent all their time hearing or telling something new,
but were, most of them, deaf to the summons and appeal of the
gospel.[35] Whenever sayings and stories from the New Testament
speak of groups of people, they raise the question whether the modern reader actually belongs to the group or is a member of a community which bears similarities to it. They also raise the question of
a possible *contrast* between the Church and the ancient group. The
Church may be unlike the ancient Church, or it may be unlike the
Pharisees, Sadducees and inhabitants of Athens. Moreover, when
the question of similarity to the early Church is raised, it is important to decide whether the similarity occurs in matters where the
conduct of the early Christians is to be commended or in matters
where it merits condemnation.

Modern readers of the Scriptures may discover other modern
groups as well as the Church, when they develop a Christian interpretation of the biblical writings. They may see similarities and
differences between their own and that of the Jewish nation or the
Romans. This kind of interpretation is to be found in the New
Testament itself, where Rome is described as Babylon and a fate is
predicted for it comparable to that which befell the city of Babylon.[36] This process of discovery need not be confined to the large

community of the nation. Smaller groups, political and social, may be discovered in the reading of the Scriptures. Industrial groups, either management or unions, may be challenged to consider if in reality they oppose Christianity because it is jeopardizing their economic ambitions. They may ask if they are like the silversmiths at Ephesus, who opposed Paul because his successful evangelism reduced the demand for the shrines which they made in honour of the goddess Artemis.[37] Modern individuals may consider if the social group to which they belong behaves like the Pharisees or the Sadducees or the tax-collectors. They may ask themselves if their attitude to Jesus is like that of the places in Galilee and Samaria which rejected him.[38] A Christian interpretation of the Scriptures is concerned to show how they bring assurance or warning or challenge to the various groups in which modern readers may find themselves.

Discovering Others

The Bible does not only provide opportunities for the discovery of Jesus, God and the self. It is also a place where other people may be encountered. The commandment 'You shall love your neighbor as yourself'[39] is not just about people in the first century. It addresses men and women in every century. There is the same agelessness about the Golden Rule with its injunction, 'So whatever you wish that men would do to you, do so to them'.[40] It is obviously concerned with conduct to men and women of every nation and every age. The other person is directly *present* in this teaching. There is no need to make a comparison between inhabitants of the modern world and inhabitants of the Roman Empire. These words of Jesus speak directly about relationships with other people today, just as clearly as they spoke about relationships with other people in Jesus's time.

Besides these general commandments which cover the whole sphere of human relationships, there are particular commandments about not being angry with one's neighbour, not passing judgement on others, and not divorcing one's spouse.[41] These commandments are not confined to men and women who lived in the first century. They challenge the present generation. The commandment about anger refers not merely to other people's behaviour to their neighbours, but to ourselves and our dealings with our neighbours. The commandment about not judging others is not only about people in the ancient world but also about ourselves and our contemporaries. The commandment about divorce is not just about married couples in Jesus's day. It is about us and our spouses and our contemporaries and their spouses.

There are also places where other people are discovered by *similarity*. They may, for example, be in a similar condition to the man left half-dead by the roadside in the parable of the Good Samaritan.[42] They are not to be directly identified with the wounded man, but may be in a position like his. The similarity may be a direct one, as in the case of someone who is physically in need of help; or it may be less direct, as with someone who is spiritually in distress. In that case there is a strong element of *contrast* mingled with the similarity. The parable challenges us to consider whether we are neglecting or attending to the needs of other people.

In his First Letter to the Corinthians Paul advises his readers to show special consideration for Christians with scruples about eating meat sacrificed to idols. He counsels them to abstain from the meat rather than jeopardize the faith of their friends.[43] The eating of meat sacrificed to idols is not an issue likely to trouble modern Christians, but Paul's words are a challenge to us to consider if some aspects of our conduct, though not wrong in principle, are causing another person's faith to be endangered.

In addition to the self, the *group* to which one belongs may be discovered in the reading of the Scriptures. Groups with commercial interests, like the Ephesian silversmiths whose trade was damaged by Paul's missionary success,[44] have their equivalents in the modern business community. The books of the New Testament raise the question of our relationship to such groups, of our attitude to the state, to the world of commerce, and to institutional religion. They lead us to consider the extent to which we should be obedient to the secular government and to the institutional Church, and to which we should be ready to disobey these authorities. They challenge us to examine how far the social, economic and political systems, in which we live, are consistent with the standards of Jesus, and they raise the issue of the ways in which we should participate in these systems.

Since the New Testament speaks of God's will for the whole universe, it is concerned with our relation not just to human beings but to the *non-human creation.* There are passages in the gospels which speak of God's concern for the birds of the air and the lilies of the field.[45] Paul writes of the longing of the whole created universe for redemption and of God's wish to reconcile all things to himself.[46] These are not central themes of the New Testament, which is primarily concerned with God's purpose for the redemption of the human race, but since God is regarded as a faithful creator, some of the New Testament writings show a belief in his desire to redeem the rest of his creation. There is little or no speculation about the details of this redemption; even the Book of Revelation with its vision of the new heaven and the new earth does not give any clue to the destiny of the animal world; but the New Testament shows a concern for that destiny, even if it does not speculate about the form which it will take. Hence a Christian interpretation of the New Testament will recognize that the whole created universe including the non-human part of it is intended by God for redemption.

Alternative Discovery-Points

In some instances the same person may be discovered at more than one point in a passage. In Jesus's sayings, for example, he himself often appears both as the authority who utters the saying, and as a person who is included in the saying. If the parable of the Feast in Matthew's Gospel is treated as an allegory, Jesus appears in two roles: first as the authority who utters the parable; then as the king's son to whose marriage feast the guests were invited. As the authority behind the parable he is discovered there by his presence. As the king's son in whose honour the feast was being held, he is discovered by similarity[47].

Another example of alternative discovery-points is found in the parable of the Good Samaritan. Readers of the parable may find a resemblance between themselves and the priest or the Levite who failed to succour the wounded man; or they may detect a likeness between themselves and the Samaritan who came to the victim's aid. They may also discover a similarity between themselves and the wounded man who was in need of help.[48]

Three points of discovery for the self may be found in the parable of the Prodigal Son. Readers may be challenged to consider if their conduct is like that of the father, who showed mercy on his wayward son. They may also discover themselves in the prodigal son who is the recipient of the father's mercy. They may even see a resemblance between themselves and the self-righteous elder son who was jealous of his brother.[49]

Where there are alternative points of discovery, one of them will sometimes take precedence over the others. The early theologians who saw the parable of the Good Samaritan as an allegorical picture of the saving activity of Jesus, read into it a meaning which was consistent with the central theme of the New Testament. Some of the details of their account were bizarre, for example, the explanation of Jerusalem as Paradise, and Jericho as this fallen world, but they rightly recognized that love for neighbour was supremely exemplified in Jesus's work of salvation, that Jesus's conduct was like the Samaritan's, and that we, like the wounded man, are in need of help.[50] Attractive as this account may be, it is not the interpretation intended by Luke, who regards the parable as an illustration of the love which one person should show for another. The obvious function of the parable is to challenge us to consider whether we are like the priest and the Levite or like the Samaritan. It does not primarily ask us to discover ourselves in the wounded man. Jesus is the authority behind the parable rather than one of the characters in it. The interpretation given by those early theologians who discover Jesus in the Samaritan and the self in the wounded man, is secondary. Since it shows Jesus as an example of the conduct which he commends to his followers, it is not to be dismissed as mistaken. It must not be allowed, however, to obscure the meaning of the parable conveyed by the biblical Jesus himself, as he is depicted in Luke's Gospel.

The Importance of the Points of Discovery

The four points of discovery which have been examined—the Jesus-point, the God-point, the self-point and the other-point—are integral to a Christian interpretation of the Scriptures. Jesus is not only the criterion by which the teaching of the Bible is understood. He is also discovered in the reading of it. He is found there by his presence or by similarity or contrast; even if he is not found in relation to one of the people in any given story, he is found as the authority behind the Scriptures. The key to a Christian interpretation of the Bible is the discovery of Jesus himself there.

Since Jesus is the revelation of God, an interpretation must also have a second point of discovery, the God-point. In a large number of instances God is to be found at the same point as Jesus, but in some instances, his discovery-point is different from that of Jesus. In stories where God addresses Jesus, like the account of his baptism, the Jesus-point and the God-point are different from each other. The same is true of the story of Jesus in Gethsemane, where he speaks to God in prayer. When Jesus heals or forgives people, however, the Jesus-point is the same as the God-point, because God is acting through him.

The third point is the self-point. Unless a passage issues a challenge or gives some assurance to the readers themselves, either as individuals or as members of a group, it is not relevant for them. If it does not evoke a response of worship or obedience from them, it has not functioned as Scripture for them. The Scriptures were written to have a direct impact on the lives of their readers.

The fourth point is the other-point. Christianity is concerned with love for neighbours and proclaims that God has a redemptive purpose for the whole universe. Few interpretations of Scripture can legitimately be confined to a purely private relationship between the self and God or Jesus Christ. Most passages of Scripture lead to a consideration of our relationship to other people, either as individuals or in groups. Some passages lead even to an examination of our relationships to the non-human parts of creation.

Christian interpretation of the New Testament takes place, when Jesus is used as the criterion and when these points of discovery are sought there. By functioning both as the criterion and as one who can be discovered, he gives us our bearings and enables us to be alert to the meaning of Scripture for the present day. Instead of just being a collection of documents of religious movements in a bygone age, the Bible is able to address us directly, and speak to us of our present relationship to Jesus Christ.

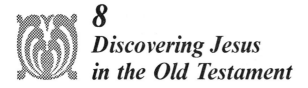

8
Discovering Jesus in the Old Testament

Jesus is to be discovered in the reading of both the Old Testament and the New Testament. Many interpreters of former times have given recognition to this important aspect of the Christian approach to the Bible. 'Everything in the Scripture', says Augustine, 'resounds Christ'.[1] 'In the whole scripture', Luther affirms, 'there is nothing else but Christ'.[2] Because the Old Testament was Christian Scripture, it had to be related to Jesus Christ. Christian interpreters were not satisfied with discerning him only in prophecies which they regarded as messianic. They also sought him in the events which the Old Testament narrated. They found him in the original act of creating the world. They found him in Moses, Joshua and David. Stories which were ostensibly about the patriarchs and rulers of Israel became, in the hands of Christian interpreters, stories about Jesus Christ.

From the point of view of historical investigation, of course, Jesus is not to be found in the Old Testament—the writers of its books did not have him in mind—but from the point of view of Christian interpreters, he has been discovered there in various ways.

One way in which he can be found is as *the fulfilment of prophecy*. Christians have claimed that he is the prophet like Moses, whom, according to the Book of Deuteronomy, God will raise up. They have argued that he is the messianic king, whose coming is foretold by the prophets. They have proclaimed him as the Suffering Servant described in the latter part of Isaiah. Such interpretation of prophecy begins in the New Testament itself, and has continued to the present day.

An objection to this explanation of prophecy is that the authors were not actually thinking of Jesus of Nazareth. For example, according to modern scholars, the author of Deuteronomy did not have Jesus in mind in foretelling the emergence of a prophet like Moses.[3] Either he was referring to a single ideal prophet, whose identity he did not know; or he was setting forward a standard to distinguish true from false prophets. If either of these explanations is correct, the words of Deuteronomy could in fact have been fulfilled by Nathan, Elijah, Amos, Hosea, Isaiah and other biblical prophets. From the Christian point of view, however, it found its true fulfilment in Jesus. He is the prophet like Moses. Such is the view of some of the New Testament writers, and such has been the view of many subsequent interpreters. This interpretation is not in conflict with the explanations given by modern Old Testament scholars. It is possible for prophecy to be fulfilled in more than one way. To a limited extent the words of Deuteronomy were fulfilled in the Hebrew prophets, but the crowning fulfilment was in Jesus.

A similar comment can be made on the various prophecies which are generally regarded as messianic. Such is the case with the well known words of Isaiah: 'For to us a child is born, to us a son is given; and the government will be upon his shoulder, and his name will be called "Wonderful Counsellor, Mighty God, Everlasting Father, Prince of Peace" '.[4] Modern scholars are divided in their opinion of the original intention of these words. Some of them think that they were not even prophetic, but were uttered in celebration of the birth or enthronement of a particular Jewish king, perhaps Hezekiah. Others believe them to have been a prophecy about an ideal king. Similar accounts can be given of Isaiah's prophecy about 'a shoot from the stump of Jesse'.[5] Originally it may have referred to a particular monarch like Hezekiah or to some ideal future king. As for Isaiah's saying about the birth of a child called Immanuel,[6] it might have originally referred to the birth of Hezekiah, or even to a future time of prosperity when parents would give the name Immanuel to their children. All these prophecies, however, have been understood by Christians to have received their fulfilment in Jesus.

Some passages, which do not appear to have been intended as prophecies, have been treated as such by Christian interpreters.

Psalm 2, for example, is thought by many scholars to have been intended to celebrate the enthronement of a Jewish king, whom it describes as the Lord's 'anointed'.[7] The words, 'You are my son, today I have begotten you',[8] are thought to refer to God's recognition of the monarch's kingship. Celebration of a royal enthronement appears also to have been the occasion of Psalm 110, with its opening lines,

> The Lord says to my Lord:
>   'Sit at my right hand,
>   till I make your enemies your footstool'.[9]

Since these psalms were not written as prophecies, Jesus cannot strictly be regarded as the fulfilment of them. On the other hand, he is the fulfilment of the ideal of kingship, which is contained in them. The qualities that were praised in earthly monarchs find their highest realization in him. The songs which celebrate their triumphs can also be used to celebrate his triumph, a point which Calvin recognized in his comments on Psalm 2.[10]

Even when a king is not mentioned in a prophecy, Jesus can be seen as the one who fulfils the Old Testament expectation. He is the bringer of the new covenant promised in Jeremiah.[11] He will establish the new heavens and the new earth foretold in the final chapters of Isaiah.[12] There is no evidence that the prophets had Jesus of Nazareth specifically in mind, but from the Christian point of view their expectations receive fulfilment in him. The noblest hopes and aspirations of Israel are realized in him.

He is also seen as the fulfilment of the Servant Songs in the second part of Isaiah.[13] Modern commentators have disagreed about the actual identity of the Servant who is mentioned in these songs. Some have seen him as a particular person. Others have understood him to be symbolic of the nation of Israel. It is not even clear whether the songs were intended as a prophecy or as an allusion to a person or persons already in existence. Within the New Testament, however, Jesus is said to be the Servant who suffers and dies to redeem the people.[14]

When there is more than one opinion about the fulfilment of a prophecy, it does not follow that only one of them can be right.

Even in the New Testament, prophecies are said to be fulfilled in more than one way. In Mark and Matthew, for example, it is indicated that John the Baptist fulfils the expectation of the return of Elijah. In various ways, however, Luke and Acts indicate that the expectation is fulfilled in Jesus. The Book of Revelation likens one of the two witnesses to Elijah.[15] It is possible for a prophecy to have two or more different fulfilments. The Old Testament predictions about the coming of a king came to partial fruition in various Judaean monarchs, but reached their true fulfilment in Jesus. Yet the fulfilment was greater than the Jews had imagined. Fulfilment transcended expectation.

Jesus is also to be discovered in the Old Testament, insofar as he is *prefigured* there. This has been a popular mode of interpretation from the earliest days of Christianity. In the New Testament itself it is indicated that he was prefigured by Adam, Jacob, Moses, David and Elijah. To say that someone prefigures Jesus is to say that he represents Jesus beforehand. It implies that there is *similarity* between the two of them. Both Adam and Jesus were in the image of God.[16] Both Jacob and Jesus could be regarded as embodiments of Israel.[17] Both Moses and Jesus established a covenant between God and human beings.[18] Both of them were liberators. Jesus, like David, was king of Israel.[19] Jesus, like Elijah, ascended into heaven. His spirit, like Elijah's, came upon his disciples.[20]

Where there is similarity, there is also *contrast*. Jesus transcends the heroes of the Old Testament. He is not only like Moses. He is greater than Moses. His teaching, says the Sermon on the Mount, is superior to that of Moses.[21] While the law was given through Moses, says John's Gospel, grace and truth came through Jesus Christ. Moses only prayed for manna in the wilderness; Jesus is the bread of life. Moses, by lifting up the serpent, obtained physical healing for the sick; Jesus was himself lifted up on the cross to give eternal life.[22] Contrast is also found in the comparison with Elijah. While Elijah called down fire on Samaritan soldiers, Jesus, according to Luke's record, refused to give the same treatment to the inhabitants of a Samaritan village.[23] There is contrast, too, between Jesus and David. Not only is there a vast moral difference between the two men, but, as Peter points out in his speech at Pentecost, David is still lying in the grave while Jesus has risen from the dead.[24] In John's Gospel a contrast is made between Jesus and Jacob. While Jacob's well supplies ordinary water, Jesus offers living water.[25] Of all the contrasts the sharpest is that which is made with Adam in the letters of Paul. Adam was disobedient to God; Jesus was obedient. Adam was only a living soul; Jesus is a life-giving spirit. Adam brought sin and death into the world; Jesus brings righteousness and life.[26]

An important example of this kind of interpretation is found in the Letter to the Hebrews, which describes Jesus as a sacrificial victim who willingly offers himself to God. Here it is the sacrificial animals who prefigure Jesus: the lambs and bulls and goats that were slaughtered on the altar.[27] Such interpretation is not confined to the Letter to the Hebrews. In the Gospels of Mark and Matthew Jesus's blood is the blood of the covenant sacrifice.[28] In John's Gospel he is the passover lamb.[29] Similar ideas are found in the Letters of Paul and Peter, the Book of Revelation and the Acts of the Apostles.[30] The thought is most fully developed, however, in Hebrews, which sees contrast as well as similarity between the sacrifice of Christ and the sacrifice of animals. While the animals were involuntary victims, Christ offered himself freely. While the animals were physically pure, Christ was morally and spiritually pure. While the animal sacrifices had to be repeated, Christ's one offering was effective for all time.[31]

This kind of interpretation is often described as typology. The Old Testament characters, Adam, Jacob, Moses, David and Elijah are the types, because they prefigure Jesus Christ. Corresponding to them is the antitype, Jesus himself, the one who is prefigured. Consistent with this mode of expression is Paul's description of Adam as 'a type of the one who was to come'.[32] Typology implies that Jesus himself is prefigured by individuals who lived in generations previous to his, and that events in which he was involved during his earthly life were prefigured by events narrated in the Old Testament, such as the Creation, the Exodus, and the entry into the Promised Land.

In principle there is nothing wrong in the search for the prefigurement of gospel events in the Old Testament. The link between the first creation and the new creation, between the old covenant and the new covenant, between Israel and the Church, and between the heroes of Israel and Jesus Christ was inherent in Christian thought from the earliest times. It is not just a method of comparison, although its blend of similarity and contrast involves comparison, nor is it just a method of illustration, although it uses the Old Testament to illustrate the New Testament. It presupposes that God was active in the creation of the universe and in the history of Israel. It implies that because God was at work in events narrated in the Old Testament, they foreshadow his activity in Jesus Christ.

The very contrasts between the Old and the New Testaments raise theological problems. Some of the actions attributed to God in the Old Testament do not harmonize with the standards of Jesus. If God is the God of love, mercy and justice, he cannot have initiated brutal massacres or sent natural disasters, which indiscriminately wiped out whole populations. He can only have been active in the creation of the world and the history of Israel in ways which are consistent with Jesus's revelation of him.

Another problem is raised by the conflict between some of the standards of the Old Testament and those of Jesus. He rejects the principle of retribution affirmed by the Jewish Law. He also rejects the idea, which is certainly present in the Old Testament, that hatred is the appropriate attitude to be shown to an enemy. It may be asked why God should have transmitted teaching through Moses, which fell below the standard revealed in Jesus Christ. One answer to this question is that God chose to educate the human race by making a gradual revelation of his will to them, and that he did not unfold to them at first the truth that they should love their enemies. Another answer to the same question is that he did not withhold truth from them, but that they failed to recognize it, so that the teaching of the Old Testament is an imperfect apprehension of his will. The Christian interpretation of the Old Testament, however, does not depend on the solution to this particular theological problem. It is possible to discover Jesus in the Old Testament by means of similarity and contrast, whatever decision is made about the extent to which God was actually responsible for the commandments recorded there.

Nor does the Christian interpretation of the Old Testament depend on the detailed historical accuracy of every statement made
there. For example, it is not necessary to believe in the literal accuracy of the story of Adam and Eve, in order to discover Jesus in the
reading of it. Basic to the Christian message is a belief in God the
creator, and a belief in the sinful state of the human race. But there
is a sense in which Adam is representative of fallen humanity, and
in that sense there is similarity and contrast between him and Jesus.
It is therefore a secondary matter whether the human race emerged
in the precise circumstances described in the Book of Genesis. From
the viewpoint of Christian faith the important feature is the similarities and differences between Adam as described in Genesis and the
biblical Jesus.

To say that Adam or Moses prefigures Jesus is not the same as
to say that accounts of their activities are actual references to him.
Such, however, was the interpretation given by some of the early
Christian theologians, and indeed by many of their successors for
numerous centuries. For example, Origen, the great third century
theologian and biblical commentator, claims that there are spiritual
and moral meanings in the Bible, which are more important than
the literal ones. In explaining the account of the battle of Jericho, he
asserts that Joshua stands for Jesus, and Jericho for this world. The
seven priests carrying trumpets represent Matthew, Mark, Luke,
John, James, Jude and Peter. The prostitute Rahab stands for the
Church, which consists of sinners; and the scarlet cord which she
displayed to save herself and her household from the massacre
stands for the redemptive blood of Christ.[33] From Origen's point of
view it is not just a question of the Fall of Jericho prefiguring the
victory of Christ over the world; the story in the Book of Joshua
actually means that Christ will win that victory.

The word 'allegory' is often used to describe this kind of interpretation of the Scriptures, and can coincide with typology, although it need not necessarily do so. Characteristic of allegory is the
attempt to squeeze hidden meaning out of every statement in the
Scriptures. For example, Origen claims that the 'people of the East',
who attacked the Israelites in the days of Gideon, represent Christian heretics, who bear the name of Christ but fight against the

Church and the Christian faith. His reason for this remarkable explanation is that 'the East' stands for Christ, a reason which itself is based on a mistaken translation of Zechariah.[34] Other examples of this kind of interpretation have been mentioned in an earlier chapter, where reference was made to the explanation of Agag as a symbol for human pride and the Babylonian infants as symbols for evil desires.[35] Commentators have shown a special dexterity in their allegorical treatment of the Song of Solomon. Originally this work was intended as a love poem, but in the Jewish interpretation it was regarded as an allegory in which the bridegroom stood for God and the bride for Israel.[36] Christians have approached the book in similar fashion, arguing that the bridegroom stands for Christ and the bride for the individual soul.[37] It is not only the main theme of the book which is treated in this way. The statement, 'The King has brought me into his chamber', Origen explains, means that Christ, the bridegroom, has brought either the Church or the individual into the chamber of his mind, to share the experience of Paul, who says, 'We have the mind of Christ'.[38]

Allegorizing interpretations of this nature fascinate the minds of some readers but provoke the hostility of others. To some students this kind of interpretation has become the medium of intense and profound spiritual experience; to others it is bizarre and even absurd, but in the study of the Scriptures it cannot be dismissed out of hand. It is not always imposed on the Bible by commentators. Sometimes it is already present in the mind of the biblical writer. It is found in Genesis, in the dreams of Joseph, Pharaoh, the royal butler and the royal baker. It occurs in the Book of Daniel, in the dreams of Nebuchadnezzar and Daniel.[39] There is allegory in the parables of Jesus, at any rate in the form in which they appear in the gospels,[40] and it is vividly exemplified in the Book of Revelation.[41] When a Scripture writer intends his words to be understood allegorically, they should be interpreted allegorically.

If it is not clear that a passage was intended as allegory, it is unwise to act on the assumption that it was. When it is treated by a commentator as allegorical, it is usually assumed to have a hidden meaning. More often than not, this is an unfounded assumption. Yet when it is interpreted allegorically, it often acquires a relevance for the present day, which it would not possess if attention were confined to its meaning in the mind of the writer. Much of the difficulty is removed, however, when it is treated as *illustration* rather than allegory. The most serious problem about allegory is not the strange and wild symbolism, in which it indulges in its extreme forms, but the implication that the writers themselves really intended their works to be understood allegorically, and that God himself willed them to have this meaning. There is no doubt that the dreams in Genesis and Daniel are intended to be interpreted allegorically, but it is highly improbable that the Song of Solomon was intended by its author to refer to the marriage of Christ to the Church or the soul; it is even less likely that the king's chamber was meant to symbolize the mind of Christ. There is no good reason to conclude that the author of the First Book of Samuel intended the account of the death of Agag as symbolical of the eradication of pride in the human soul. There is no convincing evidence that the writer of Psalm 137 meant the Babylonian infants to represent evil desires. There is no likelihood that the author of the Book of Judges intended the 'people of the East' to symbolize Christian heretics; nor is it in any way apparent that God placed these hidden meanings in the text but concealed them from the writers. Nevertheless, while it is a very speculative procedure to treat these passages allegorically, it is an entirely different matter to use them as illustrations of the Christian message. Once they are treated in this way, they are likely to have a wider acceptance than when they are interpreted as allegories. Illustrations are to be used insofar as they effectively illustrate. Otherwise they can be discarded. The illustrative appeal of passages like those which have been mentioned will vary from person to person. It is unlikely that Origen's account of 'the people of the East' will have a widespread appeal. The use of the Song of Solomon to illustrate Christ's relationship to his people is likely to receive wider appreciation, provided the temptation is resisted to unveil a symbolical meaning in every verse. Illustration is a more satisfactory approach than allegory, except where the biblical writer obviously intended his work to be interpreted allegorically.

Jesus can also be discovered in the Old Testament *where God is mentioned.* The New Testament writers are well aware of this possibility. Some of them claim that Christ was active in the creation of the universe.[42] Others see him as present with the Israelites in the wilderness and appearing to Isaiah in the Temple.[43] The precise meaning of these assertions about his activity before his physical birth are a matter of theological debate. They clearly indicate, however, that the activity of God in creation and in the history of Israel was also the activity of Christ. If these insights are accepted, it is possible to find Jesus in the very places where God is found in the Old Testament, but when he is discovered there, an element of contrast will sometimes emerge between his revelation of God, and the understanding of God conveyed by the Old Testament writers.

Jesus interprets the Scriptures by enabling us to discover himself there. Such was the insight of Charles Wesley when he wrote.

> Jesus, divine Interpreter,
>   To me thine oracles unseal,
> Then shall I find and taste thee there,
>   Thy truth, and power, and mercy feel,
> And nothing know, and nothing see
> In all the book of God but thee.[44]

Like many people before him, Charles Wesley made a free use of the allegorical method of interpretation, but even when a firm restraint is put on such a method, it is possible to discover Jesus in the Bible, in both the Old and the New Testament. As the interpreter, Jesus not only acts as the criterion, measuring the Scriptures by his standard, but also allows himself to be found there. Through prophecy and prefigurement and through presence, similarity and contrast, he can be encountered in the Bible. It is an exaggeration to say that we see and know there nothing but him. Yet when he is the interpreter, nothing is known or seen in the Bible except in relation to him. The Scriptures themselves are viewed in his light; God is revealed there by him; and we discover both ourselves and others there through him.

9
Letting the Old Testament Speak for Today

In a Christian interpretation of the Old Testament, there are, as in the interpretation of the New Testament, four discovery-points, that is, places where Jesus, God, the self, and others may be found. Because of the special problems related to the discovery of Jesus in pre-Christian Scriptures, a separate chapter has been devoted to that theme. There are, however, the three other discovery-points to discuss in relation to the interpretation of the Old Testament. If it is to be relevant for the present day, God, the self and others must be found there as well as Jesus.

Discovering God

God is present on almost every page of the Old Testament. He created the world, drove Adam and Eve from Eden, sent the flood on the earth, preserved Noah and his family, and sent Abraham into the Promised Land. He chose the Israelites to be his people, delivered them from captivity in Egypt, gave them the Law, guided them through their history, blessed them when they were obedient and punished them when they were disobedient.

From the Christian point of view, the God of the Old Testament is the same as the God of the New Testament. Jesus himself sees no discontinuity between the God of the Hebrew Scriptures and the God whom he reveals. His God is the God of Abraham, Isaac and Jacob. He does not entertain the idea that the God of Israel is any other than the God whom he makes known.

It is therefore God himself, who is discovered in the Old Testament. He is discovered there by his *presence*. However, the account of his activities and of his characteristics is not always consistent with that which is given through the revelation in Jesus Christ. The Old Testament accounts of the behaviour of God are subject to the judgement of Jesus himself. The God revealed by Jesus would not have ordered that Agag, the king of the Amalekites, should be slaughtered in cold blood. He would not have commanded the Israelites to murder a large proportion of the Midianite women and make captives of the rest of them. There is a contrast between some of the Old Testament accounts of God and Jesus's revelation of him. With Jesus as interpreter, it is recognized not only that God revealed himself through many of the teachings of the Old Testament, and that God was active in many of the leaders and prophets of Israel and Judah, but also that many of the Old Testament teachings are inconsistent with the revelation of God in Jesus, and that many of the actions said to have been performed at his command, could not have been willed by the God of love and justice. God is present in the Old Testament, but the Old Testament accounts of God show a mixture of *similarity* and *contrast*, when they are compared with the revelation of him by the biblical Jesus.

Discovering Ourselves

In most passages of the Old Testament there is a place for the discovery of the self. Just as the New Testament writings for the most part had early Christians in mind and not Christians of later generations, so for the most part the Old Testament writers had in mind their own contemporaries and not the members of future civilizations. Their message was directed chiefly to Israelites and sometimes to the inhabitants of surrounding countries. They did not think of people living many centuries ahead of them. Nevertheless modern readers can find connections between themselves and people mentioned in the Old Testament. They may discover themselves as they read about individual characters in a narrative. Or they may discover themselves as the persons to whom a commandment or warning or word of assurance is addressed.

The self can be discovered insofar as it participates in the *fulfilment of prophecy*. Readers of Isaiah can discover themselves in the people who walked in darkness and saw a great light.[1] In the words 'for to us a child is born',[2] they can see themselves in the men and women for whom the child is to come. Insofar as Jesus is regarded as the Suffering Servant, the self can be discovered amongst the men and women for whose transgressions he was wounded, and whose sin he bore.[3] Prophecies about new heavens and a new earth[4] can be interpreted as having their fulfilment when the self participates in the new creation. The self can also find its place in the prophecy of a new covenant.[5] The original prophecy had Israel and Judah in mind, but Christians, regarding the Church as the people of God, can say that they are the people with whom the new covenant has been made.

Modern readers may discover themselves in the Old Testament insofar as they are *prefigured* by the people of Israel. From the Christian point of view, Israel prefigured the Church. At different stages in history both Israel and the Church have functioned as the people of God. Both are said in the Bible to have been chosen by God. Both are recipients of warnings, challenges, assurances and promises from God. Hence there is *similarity* between them. Christians, therefore, in reading the Old Testament, can look for similarities between themselves and the Israelites. They can consider if their own behaviour is like that which is commended or denounced in the nation of Israel. They can ask if they show the same kind of loyalty or disloyalty to God. They can also discover themselves by *contrast* with the people of Israel, perceiving that their own behaviour differs in various respects from that of the Israelites.

In reacting to the Jewish Law we may find a similarity between ourselves and the Israelites. The great commandments about love for God and love for neighbour[6] speak directly to our situation as well as to theirs. Indeed they speak with such immediacy that we may well discover ourselves by *presence* as the very people to whom they are addressed. Such an approach would be supported by the way in which Jesus placed these two commandments at the centre of his own teaching, and addressed them to his own disciples. Sometimes, however, the commandments of the Jewish Law are unacceptable to a Christian. Since Jesus himself rejected the principle of retribution, 'An eye for an eye and a tooth for a tooth',[7] Christian readers cannot appropriately find themselves among the people addressed by these words. The Church and the people of Israel live under two different covenants. In reading the Old Testament principle of retribution, Christians discover themselves as people who live under a covenant which is different from that which was established through Moses. The ritual laws of the Old Testament provide further examples of commandments, which have been superseded by the new covenant inaugurated by Jesus Christ. In some cases, there is little to be said about these ritual laws except that they have been superseded. Yet sometimes it is possible to discover a Christian message by reflecting on them. The laws about sacrifice remind the Christian that Jesus himself has offered the effective sacrifice for men and women. They also may bring to mind the words of Paul about the offering of the self as a sacrifice to God, and the reference in the Letter to the Hebrews about offering sacrifices of praise, thanksgiving and good works.[8]

We can also find ourselves in individual men and women of the Old Testament. There is an obvious similarity between modern human beings and Adam and Eve. They are all created by God and they are all disobedient to God. However many difficulties we may encounter in the stories of Creation and the Fall, the relevance of these stories to the present situation is abundantly clear. They tell of God's purpose for men and women to live in obedience to him. They tell of the tragedy of human separation from him and rebellion against him.

It is always possible for modern readers to find *similarity* and *contrast* between themselves and individuals mentioned in the Old Testament. The leading men and women in Israel's history present a powerful mixture of virtue and vice. We can consider whether we resemble them in their most or their least commendable features. We can ask whether we are like David in his courage and readiness to repent, or in his selfishness and immorality.[9] We can consider whether the self is to be discovered in Joshua's fearless energy, his commitment to a cause, his sense of divine mission, or in his ruthlessness and brutality;[10] whether it is to be found in Deborah's courageous leadership or in her approval of Jael's grisly murder of Sisera.[11] We can ask whether the self is to be found in Jacob's readiness to serve God or in his deceitfulness to his father and his brother;[12]

whether it is to be discovered in Abraham's trust in God and obedience to his will, or in his willingness to let his wife be taken into Pharaoh's harem in order to preserve his own life.[13] It is also possible to discover the self in people other than members of the nation of Israel. We may find ourselves in the arrogance of Nebuchadnezzar, or the hard-heartedness of Pharaoh.[14] All these are places where, by similarity or contrast, there is an opportunity for self-discovery.

When people discover themselves in the Old Testament, they receive an abundant supply of challenge, warning and promise. They may also find assurance that God can use them in spite of their shortcomings. The Old Testament provides evidence of God's readiness to use imperfect agents, to work through men and women who have been disloyal to him and disobeyed his commandments. Even though Sarah was jealous and defective in faith, God blessed her with a child.[15] Even though David sinned in his treatment of Uriah and his adultery with Bathsheba, God continued to use him as his servant. Besides all the warnings of divine judgement, there are assurances that God can work through men and women in spite of their moral and spiritual weakness.

In the Old Testament, as in the New Testament, the self may be found as a member of a *group*. The idea of the group has already been mentioned in describing the prefiguration of the Church by the people of Israel. The most obvious approach to this aspect of discovery is to consider whether the present day Church is similar to or different from the nation of Israel in biblical times. But it is also possible to examine other groups of men and women, for example, the Egyptians or the Assyrians or the Babylonians, and to consider whether their virtues and vices are in any way shared by the present-day Church. Since, however, the Old Testament is mainly concerned with the people of Israel, there are more opportunities to discover the self in them than in other peoples. As we read of that nation's history and hear the warnings and promises of the prophets to them, we can let those challenges and assurances speak to us; we can let ourselves be drawn into the circle of the Old Testament stories, and discover ourselves as we read them.

It is not just as the recipients of challenges, promises and commandments that the self can be discovered in the Old Testament. We can share in the moments of experience of the presence of God which are recorded there. We can be with Jacob as he sees a vision of angels or as he wrestles with God. We can share with Moses the awe and wonder of God's presence at the burning bush or on the mountain. We can be with Isaiah as he confronts God in fear and trembling in the Temple, or with Ezekiel as he receives his strange vision of divine glory.[16] Though we may not share the full intensity of the experiences described, we can still be enriched by them and find them a means of receiving an awareness of the divine presence. The discovery of the self in these places may also lead to the discovery of God.

Discovering Others

Once the self has been found in a passage of Scripture, the other person can be sought there. There is not a point of discovery for the other person in every part of the Bible; some passages deal only with the individual's relationship to God, but usually there is a place for other people too. The search for the places where others may be discovered in the Old Testament is not greatly different from the corresponding search in the New Testament. It is important to discern the similarities and contrasts between people in the modern world and people in ancient Israel. The needy, the poor, and the socially oppressed have their counterparts in modern society. Rulers, good and bad, today resemble rulers, good and bad, in Israel. There were malicious and generous people, then, as there are malicious and generous people now. Of course, theirs was a different culture from that of the modern world, and differences are not hard to discern. Moreover, they lived under the covenant of the Jewish Law, and attitudes are commended in the Old Testament, which though they may be acceptable in areas of modern society, are contrary to the teaching of Jesus. The Old Testament, however, has the advantage of recording a greater variety of situations and relationships than does the New Testament. The New Testament contains the writings of a persecuted minority which met with sharp opposition both in Palestine and in the rest of the Roman Empire. The Old Testament, however, in addition to recording the experiences of people in persecution and captivity, deals with the varying fortunes of a nation during many centuries of its history. It speaks of relationships between different classes of society, and of the involvement of God's people in political affairs. Because the servants of God are often in positions of authority and wealth, the duty of the rich and powerful is confronted in more detail in the Old Testament than in the New Testament. Within the Old Testament the other individuals and the other groups are discovered in a wide variety of situations.

There are references also in the Old Testament, as in the New Testament, to God's intention for the *non-human creation*. There are prophecies of a new heaven and a new earth. There are expectations of a world in which animals will no longer prey on each other, where the wolf will dwell with the lamb, and the leopard will lie down with the kid. God has a purpose, not disclosed in detail, which embraces the whole created universe. In such passages it is not just human beings who are discovered as the others with whom we have relationships. At the 'other-point' there may also be found the world of animals, of vegetation, and even of inanimate objects. God is the creator of the universe, and has a purpose of redemption for his creation. Within the Scriptures it is possible to discover the non-human elements of that universe and to find there challenges and promises about our relationships to them. While there are many parts of the Old Testament which give the impression that the rest of the universe exists solely for the benefit of the human race, there are other parts which envisage a future in which other creatures exist in their own right. It is this latter outlook which is the more consistent with the teaching of the biblical Jesus, for whom the birds of the air, the lilies of the field, and the sparrow that falls to the ground, had a value in God's sight apart from their service to the human race.[17] This outlook of Jesus should determine a Christian interpretation of the passages of the Old Testament where we encounter the non-human creation.

Alternative Discovery Points

In one and the same story of the Old Testament it is possible to have different sets of discovery-points. In the account of David's fight with Goliath, for example, the self may be discovered in David, and the enemy with whom we fight, may be the various obstacles encountered in daily life. These obstacles may be actual people, especially if they hinder us from carrying out God's will; or they may be handicaps which beset us, like poverty of lack of education or physical disabilities; or they could be our own besetting sins, whether they are pride or lust or greed.[18] In all these ways we may be challenged by the story of David and Goliath to combat the forces which hinder us from obedience to God. We may also find in that story an assurance that in God's strength we, like David, can overcome these forces in spite of the appearance that all odds are against us. In this interpretation of the story David is the discovery-point for the self, Goliath for the forces against which the self combats. Both Jesus and God are to be found in the Lord who delivers Goliath into the hand of David.

Another set of discovery-points can be found in the same story. Instead of being discovered in God, Jesus can be discovered in David. He is then regarded as the saviour, who, like David, frees God's people from their enemies. According to this pattern of interpretation the self is discovered not in David but in the Israelites who are powerless to defeat the Philistine but rely on David for victory. In the same way we are conscious of our own inability to save ourselves from sin and of our need to rely on the power of Jesus. The obstacles to be overcome can still be the same as in the other pattern of interpretation. They are the human opponents or physical handicaps or sinful tendencies which prevent the self from fulfilling God's purposes. When these discovery-points are established, the story tells us that, like the Israelites, we are powerless in the face of our enemies until Jesus, like David, brings us divine deliverance.

Neither of these systems of interpretation was originally intended by the author of the First Book of Samuel, who was concerned to glorify David and to tell of God's championship of Israel, but a Christian interpretation does not rest content with the original intention of the author. It lets the light of Jesus Christ shine on the ancient story in order that it may speak with its challenges and assurances to the present.

Other points of discovery can also be found in the story of David and Bathsheba.[19] The self can be discovered in David, who in the first part of the story exemplifies the vice of selfish lust. He sacrifices the life of Uriah in order to satisfy his own sexual passions. Few people will be placed in a situation where they are tempted to have somebody killed in order to indulge their sexual desires, but they may be tempted to be cruel to others and to take advantage of them, in order to indulge their own lust. They may also be tempted to harm them for desires other than sexual. In all these ways the self can be discovered by similarity to David. The points where the other person is discovered are Bathsheba and Uriah, who illustrate the way in which people are used by the self for its own ends. Yet this is a story not just of human passion and treachery, but also of divine judgement and mercy, in which the spokesman for God is the prophet Nathan. The point where God and Jesus are discovered therefore is Nathan, and the story challenges sinners to respond as David did with an acknowledgment of their sins.

The same narrative can be interpreted in a different way. The self may be discovered by similarity to Nathan, who courageously spoke God's word to the king, confronting him with his offence. It is then David who assumes the position of the other to whom the self is related, and the story is not a challenge to people to resist temptation or to repent of the evil they have done. It now challenges the Christian to be resolute in standing up for God's truth. God and Jesus are not to be found in a person in the story but are presupposed as the authority behind Nathan's words.

The conspicuous difference between the two types of approach which have been outlined is in the point of discovery for Jesus. In one style of interpretation he is to be found by his likeness to a character in the story, to David or to Nathan. In another he is to be found as the authority and power behind the events. Both these interpretations are possible. Both can convey a relevant message. In both of them there is an element of prefiguration. When David is regarded the champion of Israel against Goliath he prefigures the self as a member of the Church. When he is the saviour who comes to the help of the Israelites, he prefigures Jesus. When he sins against Uriah, he is a prefigurement of the members of the Christian community insofar as they are disobedient to God.

The approach to Old Testament interpretation which has been

outlined does not exclude the need for biblical criticism. It is important to understand the meaning of the Old Testament writings in the situations for which they were written. It is important to know how they illuminate the history of the periods which they describe and the periods in which they were written. It is important to examine them as works of literature. Christian interpretation, however, goes a step further. It looks for the discovery of Jesus, of God, of the self and of others in the study of these writings. It uses Jesus as the criterion for measuring the conduct which the writings advocate and the vision of God which they communicate. It lets Jesus himself be the interpreter.

This kind of interpretation also presupposes that God was active in the life of Israel and was responsible for the creation of the world. The truth of the Christian message does not stand or fall by the literal accuracy of every narrative in the Old Testament. It assumes that he is at work in Israel and in the universe but only in ways consistent with his revelation in Jesus Christ. The Old Testament is not just a storehouse of pictorial representations of eternal truth, nor is it just a backdrop which enables the Christian gospel to be delineated with clarity. The accounts of Jesus in the New Testament presuppose that God used the nation of Israel to prepare the way for his coming, and that the expectations of the Old Testament reached their true fulfilment in him. The books of the Old Testament bear witness to God's activity in the world and especially in the life of Israel. They also bear a witness of prophecy, expectation and promise, which the Christian recognizes as receiving fulfilment in Jesus Christ. Both these aspects of the witness of the Old Testament are acknowledged when Jesus acts as its interpreter. It is admitted that God cannot be responsible for all the actions and attitudes ascribed to him in the Old Testament. It is also recognized that in spite of this limitation the Old Testament is a field for encounter with God as revealed in Jesus Christ.

10
Where People Go Wrong

The approach to the Bible which has been outlined leaves considerable latitude for interpretation. When the relevance of a Scripture passage for the present day is examined in the light of the biblical Jesus, there can be several different systems of discovery points, and therefore several interpretations. Where there is variety of interpretation, there is also the danger of misinterpretation. Students of the Bible are liable to allow it to mean whatever suits their own inclination. While Jesus is claimed as the authority, in fact he can be used as a facade for the presentation of views which are basically opposed to him.

Since Christianity is a religion of the Spirit and not of the letter, a degree of variety is to be expected in the interpretation of the Scriptures. When freedom is granted to individuals to give expression to their own understanding of Christianity, there is bound to be a subjective element in the interpretation. There is a precedent for this subjectivity within the Bible itself. Its books have different authors with different literary styles, different interests and emphases, and different ways of expressing their beliefs. The fact that the Bible is accepted as Christian Scripture is evidence in itself that variety of interpretation is of the essence of Christianity.

Subjectivity needs to be kept within bounds, however, if the Scriptures are to be read responsibly. In an age when attempts have been made to present a Christianity without God or without hope for life after death, or a Christianity with hardly any recognizable connection with the moral teaching of the New Testament, it is important to discover the limits, beyond which an interpretation becomes a denial of the gospel. Subtle explanations of the message often make those limits difficult to discern. The rejection of the gospel can easily masquerade as its acceptance. What appears to be reinterpretation of the gospel may be in fact a denial of it. It is important, therefore, to examine some of the ways in which interpretation may go astray.

Insignificant Levels of Generality

Interpretation can be fundamentally distorted when the gospel is expressed in terms that are so general as to be insignificant. The language used is an ambiguous void which can be filled with whatever content the writer or reader wishes. The catchwords of philosophy and psychology are applied to Jesus at so general a level that he can be quoted in support of a variety of ways of life which may be totally unrelated to him.

An example is the way in which he can be described as one who has *authentic existence*, a phrase borrowed from existentialist philosophy. Merely to describe Jesus as one who exists authentically is not to make any serious contribution to the understanding of him. No doubt Nero regarded his own existence as authentic, and no doubt in later ages Casanova and Al Capone thought that they existed authentically. None of these men had the same understanding of existence as Jesus. To link Jesus with authentic existence gives no distinctive account of him until further explanation has been given. Unless it is clearly related to the style of life advocated and practised by Jesus, 'authentic existence' is merely a slogan to elicit approval for the preferences of the person who has introduced the term. It can be used in such a way as to distort rather than clarify the gospel.

Similar ambiguity arises from the use of the terms *person* and *personhood*. Jesus can be held up as the model of 'true personhood', the 'real person'. Yet these phrases convey very little meaning unless further account is given of them. It is only when more details are provided that the words begin to acquire meaning. It is very easy to say that Jesus is the model of true personhood and then to fit him into any pattern we choose to give him. To make a general comment of this nature without explaining it in terms of the life of Jesus is to leave the way open for gross misinterpretation of him. When the attainment of personhood is set forward as the goal of life, it is often no more than a cloak for the intention to pursue one's own interest. It is a goal which need have nothing to do with Christian discipleship as long as it is understood at an insignificant level of generality.

The terms *self-fulfilment* and *self-realization* are excellent examples of slogans which can be bandied about at so general a level that they can mean anything that a person desires them to mean. The realization of the true self as the aim in life is by no means to be despised. But unless some clear indication is given of the characteristics of the true self, discussion about its fulfilment or realization is empty talk. It is another instance of ambiguous terminology, which is profound in sound but shallow in content.

Even the words of the New Testament can be used in so general a sense that they are almost denuded of meaning. The word *freedom* is an example. Jesus can be described as the supremely 'free' man who gives 'freedom' to others. To depict him, however, as free without indicating the kind of freedom which he enjoys is to give an insignificant account of him. Hitler was a free man—free from the power of the law and free from the normal restraints of human conscience. If he were to be regarded merely as free, without regard for the kind of freedom which he exercised, he could be classified along with Jesus as an example of a free man. All men and women can be regarded as free in one sense or another. Even slaves who are legally bound to their owners and are regarded as pieces of property, are free to think their own thoughts. The description of Jesus as free or as one who sets others free does not distinguish him from other people. Only when specific account is given of the nature of the freedom he both enjoys and gives does the description acquire importance. As long as it fails to proceed beyond the general assertion that he is free, it remains insignificant. It is easy also to speak of *liberation* without indicating what kind of liberation is meant. There is the liberation enjoyed by the tyrant, who is bound by no law. There is the liberation of the libertine, who rejects Christian standards of morality. There is the liberation of the agnostic, who is not committed to any religious belief. None of these is consistent with

Christian discipleship, in which freedom is to be enjoyed within the boundaries set by the acceptance of Jesus as the Lord and consequently of certain standards of conduct and certain beliefs about God. The mere assertion that a person is free remains insignificant, until an account is given of the nature of that freedom.

The description of Jesus as one who enables people to be *born again* can also be an umbrella under which a host of different styles of life can shelter, many of which are fundamentally opposed to Jesus. When Dr. Jekyll was transformed into Mr. Hyde, he experienced a new beginning in life of so drastic a nature that it would have been possible to say that he had been born again. People have been converted away from Christianity as well as converted to it, but when the New Testament writers refer to being 'born again',[1] they are speaking of the beginning of the Christian life; there is sufficient precision in their accounts of that life for the idea of new birth to have distinctive meaning.

Even statements about *love* do not acquire significance, until they are related to the pattern of Jesus's life and to the whole of his teaching. Jesus's love for men and women was not of the same order as the miser's love for money or the dictator's love of power. It had its roots in a care for others which led to self-sacrifice. 'Love' is a word which can be used for a variety of life-styles, and until it is defined in terms of a distinctive pattern of life, it does not acquire meaning. Christian love is to be discovered in the life and teaching of Jesus, as depicted in the New Testament.

Insignificant treatment can also be given to the theme of *eternal life*. Until it is made clear whether it refers to everlasting life or to a life of a new quality or to both, it has little or no meaning, and when reference is made to a new quality of life, it has little significance, until it is related directly to the quality of life advocated and exemplified by Jesus himself. As for the assertion that eternal life is everlasting, it remains highly ambiguous, until it is explained whether it refers to a life that is conscious or not. The affirmation that Jesus Christ is eternally alive, for example, has little significance, until it is explained how he is alive. It can mean that he is alive solely through his influence and through the perpetuation of his teaching in the Christian tradition; or it can mean that he is alive because he came to life again after his physical death and has a conscious existence today. Many deceased people are unquestionably alive in the former of these senses, because they live through the perpetuation of their memory or the continuation of their influence. To say that Jesus is alive in this sense is to state the obvious. It is important to know whether the statement that he is alive is meant as a platitude or as an assertion of something dramatic and different about him. Unfortunately some modern exponents of Christianity intend it as a platitude.

A variety of phrases and words have been mentioned which can easily be interpreted at an insignificant level of generality. Authentic existence, person or personhood, self-fulfilment or self-realization, freedom or liberation, new birth, love and eternal life are terms which, because of their ambiguity, can easily be used as vehicles for ideas, which have little to do with the Christian message. Once they are provided with content, and once a clear indication is given of the kind of life which they signify, it will be evident whether or not they are consistent with the biblical Jesus. As long as they are presented at an insignificant level or generality, however, they can be a source of distortion and misinterpretation of the biblical message.

Acceptance of Rejected Options

Another way in which interpretation can be distorted is when viewpoints are accepted as Christian which were rejected by Jesus. The most conspicuous example of this mistake is in the treatment of the *future life*. Jesus rejected the Sadducees' teaching that there is no resurrection.[2] In opposing the views of the Sadducees he was rejecting a viewpoint which was fully available to Jews of his day. If Jesus had wished to propound a view of life, which excluded a future hope, he would not have had to break away from the conventions of Jewish thought. His environment did not force him to hope for a life after death. Many of his contemporaries in Palestine rejected it, and the Hebrew Scriptures contained little evidence to support it.[3] The majority of the Hebrew writers lived without such an expectation, their hopes being confined to developments in human history rather than to destinies which awaited individuals after their physical demise. The most that individuals could hope for was that their names would be perpetuated by their descendants[4]—a view of life which was available to Jesus and his followers, but which they chose to reject.

An account of Jesus, which sees the future merely in terms of this life, is being unfaithful to the biblical portrait of him. It is legitimate to interpret his teaching in modern terms, but to do it in such a way as to reverse its basic thrust is not interpretation but denial. There are two explanations of the future hope which are so misleading as to amount to a denial of it. The first of them is the description of it merely in terms of political and social developments, as though the Christian hope was synonymous with the expectation of a brave and prosperous new world. The second misleading explanation is the claim that eternal life is no more than a new quality of life in the present. These are gross distortions of the teaching of Jesus. He was not proclaiming a faith in the future of the human, political and social community, when he denied the Sadducees' teaching. He was not just affirming the validity of the present, when he dissociated himself from the denial of the after-life. He was affirming a belief in a future beyond this present existence.

Jesus's rejection of the Sadducees' teaching about the future is reinforced by other writings of the New Testament. In his First Letter to the Corinthians Paul says that our faith is vain if Christ is not risen, and that if our hope is for this life only, we are of all people the most pitiable.[5] Almost every book of the New Testament affirms a belief in Jesus as risen, and most of them explicitly look forward to a future life. Central to the early Church's message was the belief in Jesus's resurrection as an affirmation of a destiny beyond this life.

Even when the Christian message was launched into a non-Jewish environment, encountering the numerous religions and philosophies in the Hellenistic world, it did not mute its call to a belief in a hereafter. Epicureans, Sceptics, many of the Stoics, and numerous other inhabitants of the Roman world refused to commit themselves to any hope for a life to come. If the early Christians had not believed this hope to be an essential part of their message, they could have allowed it to disappear without feeling any contrary pressure from the prevailing spirit of the age.

The rejection of the Sadducees' viewpoint is vividly presented in the first three gospels and is confirmed by the general consensus of New Testament teaching. Any modern theology, which sides with the Sadducees, implies that they knew better than Jesus and were able to give a more judicious appraisal than was Jesus of the limits of human destiny. To join the Sadducees in their disavowal of the hereafter is to reject Jesus Christ. Any interpretation of Christianity which agrees with the Sadducees is a denial of the gospel.

Other rejected options are found by an examination of *Jesus's attitude to conduct*. There were many patriotic Jews who wanted him to assume the role of a violent national deliverer. The gospels are in total agreement that he refused to accept that role. He rejected the attempt to make him king.[6] He counseled his followers not to use violence against their persecutors, told them to pay their taxes and accept tasks imposed upon them by the established authorities.[7] Although there was constant pressure on him to take up arms to defend his cause, he resisted that pressure even in the final days of his life when the conspiracy against him came to a head.[8] The option of *violence* was rejected by him.

A rejected option does not set as clear a limit in ethical matters as it does with belief about life after death. A change in situation does not alter the legitimacy of belief in life after death. If such a life was a possibility in the first century, it is equally a possibility in any other century. Ethical questions, on the other hand, have to be treated differently. Although violent revolution was rejected by first-century Christians, it could conceivably be appropriate action in a different situation. The total impression of Jesus, however, is of a man who avoided the use of violence and instructed his disciples not to resist persecution by force. He gave no ready-made answer to problems of war and peace or of law enforcement, but the direction of the Christian answer is indicated. Reconciliation must be preferred to violence. Jesus's token show of force in the cleansing of the Temple[9] should not be allowed to obscure the fact that his normal policy was to reject the use of violence. It is not clear that his command not to resist evil, but turn the other cheek,[10] was intended for every occasion of physical violence; but whether or not he wished it to apply to all these situations, it clearly indicates that recourse to violence is not normal Christian behaviour.

Another rejected option was *a permissive sex ethic*. It is sometimes suggested that the changed situation of the modern age warrants a change in sexual morality, and that the sexual ethic of Jesus and the early church is now outmoded. A look at the habits of the first-century Roman Empire will quickly dispel the illusion that the situation of the modern world is greatly different from that of the ancient world. Sexual promiscuity was widespread in the Roman Empire. Many couples cohabited without marriage. Adultery was often committed, and the divorce rate was extremely high. Homosexual acts were frequently practised. Even in Palestine, in spite of the traditional Jewish concern for morality, marital infidelity was by no means unknown. John the Baptist's crowning offence was to challenge the morality of Herod Antipas and his family,[11] and the presence of people described as sinners among the acquaintances of Jesus[12] implies that there was plenty of immorality in the country. Although Jesus befriended immoral persons, he never condoned their activity. Fornication and adultery were clearly denounced by him.[13] In words spoken to an adulteress, which were not in the earliest text of the gospels but still represent his attitude, he says, 'Neither do I condemn you'; but also adds, 'Go and do not sin again'.[14] He showed friendship and mercy to sinners,[15] but regarded their extra-marital sexual activity as sinful. His opposition to sexual laxity was consistent with that of traditional Judaism.[16] Even though he differed from the scribes and Pharisees in extending friendship to sinners, he did not abandon the moral standards of his people.

The strictness of Jesus's sex ethic is to be seen in his attitude to divorce. Marriage, he taught, was a lifelong institution, never to be sundered by human initiative.[17] In the country in which he lived there were two main views about the permissibility of divorce and remarriage. The school, which followed the Rabbi Shammai, claimed that divorce was allowed only on the ground of immoral conduct. In the Book of Deuteronomy it was stated that a man could divorce his wife, if he found some indecency in her.[18] Shammai said that the indecency was immorality. A laxer view was taken by the school of Hillel, which regarded dislike for a wife's cooking as an adequate reason for divorce.[19] According to Matthew, Jesus agreed with the school of Shammai, permitting divorce on grounds of immorality.[20] If Luke, Mark and Paul[21] are right, however, he was stricter than both the main schools of rabbis, being opposed to divorce under any circumstances. In a world in which he had the option of taking a lax attitude to divorce, he took a strict position, much to the embarrassment of many of his followers in the twentieth century.

Jesus also rejected the option of taking *a purely external attitude to the Jewish law.* He attempted to penetrate behind the letter of the law to its inner spirit, a procedure which resulted in the rejection of several important alternatives of conduct which were available to the Jews of his time. The Sermon on the Mount is a clear guide to the options which he rejected. It would have been possible for him to accept the command about murder merely as a prohibition of the destruction of physical life. Jesus saw it, however, as a prohibition of anger and insults as well as actual murder.[22] He rejected the option of taking the commandment only at its literal value. In dealing with the law about adultery he took a similar attitude, refusing to confine its meaning to the outward act and extending it to include a prohibition of lust.[23]

A Christian interpretation cannot acquiesce in viewpoints which Jesus rejected, unless special reasons can be given why a changed situation justifies it. Since Jesus does not deal with minute details and does not take into account the complexities of individual cases, flexibility is needed in the interpretation of his teaching, but flexibility is different from total rejection. If an interpretation does not move in the same direction as Jesus's teaching, it is a rejection of it.

Special emphasis must be placed on Jesus's rejection of the *exclusivism of scribes and Pharisees,* who ostracized tax-collectors and sinners from the social life of the community. His basic attitude is expressed in his exhortation to love enemies as well as neighbours.[24] It is supported by the parable of the Good Samaritan[25] which shows that neighbourliness transcends national barriers. While the first three gospels mention that it was Jesus's policy to confine his ministry to Jews, they recognize that he deviated from that policy by healing a Gentile girl and ministering to Samaritans.[26] He is said to have commissioned his disciples to go to the Gentiles, a mission which is probably prefigured by the mission of the seventy and the feeding of the four thousand.[27] In John's Gospel Jesus bridges the gap between Jew and Samaritan and affirms that he will draw all people to himself.[28] He is the shepherd, whose flock includes Gentiles as well as Jews.[29] God loves the whole world and sent him to save it.[30] Salvation is not limited to the physical descendants of Abraham.[31]

These options which Jesus rejected give a clue to some of the main directions of his thought. By denying the Sadducean hopelessness about the future, the Zealot desire for violent revolt, the permissive sex ethic of many of his contemporaries, the external attitude to the law adopted by many of the scribes and Pharisees and their persistent exclusivism, he was already making clear the trends of his teaching. The acceptance of these rejected options is a rejection of his teaching. It is not an interpretation but a denial of the gospel.[32]

11
Smorgasbord Theology

One of the root causes of misinterpretation is the practice of a theology which assumes the Christian religion to be free from teachings which may be distasteful to the believer. It is a theology which accepts and rejects doctrines, according to the theologian's likes and dislikes. It is reminiscent of the Scandinavian meal known as smorgasbord, where a variety of meats, fish, vegetables and spices are spread on a table. People fill their plates with the foods, which they like, and pass over those which dislike. It is a buffet meal, very convenient for individuals with a strong aversion to particular dishes, since it enables them to reject uncongenial food without drawing attention to themselves. The behaviour of participants in a smorgasbord is like the practice of many people in formulating their theology. They take what they like, and reject what they dislike.

By its very nature smorgasbord theology appears in many forms. Usually it accepts the belief that God is love and that Jesus exemplifies God's love. It also accepts Jesus's commandments about love of God and love of neighbour. Beyond that, it can be found in a variety of combinations. It leads some people to reject the doctrine that Jesus is uniquely related to God, and others to overlook any suggestion that the work of Jesus was uniquely effective in bringing about the forgiveness of sins. It leads some people to neglect the hope of a future life, others to dismiss warnings of a future judgement, and yet others to disregard the teaching that God's activity in history will reach a great consummation. It also leads people to neglect the standards of conduct taught by Jesus. It prompts them to avoid the challenge of his teaching about violence or wealth or sex. It even allows them to overlook his emphasis on the need to minister to others. It leads some people to have a theology without any emphasis on the personal nature of God and others to neglect any mention of the deep-rooted human need for forgiveness. In whichever form it appears, smorgasbord theology contains some elements of the Christian gospel but rejects others.

The Rejection of Distasteful Aspects of the Gospel

Most, if not all, Christians yield in some measure to the inclination to reject aspects of the gospel which they find to be distasteful. Yet if Christianity is a revealed religion, acceptance should be given to its message, even when it seems to be uncongenial. People do not profess Christianity with seriousness and sincerity, unless they have already found it to be attractive. A strong and stable Christian faith proceeds from a willing acceptance of the claims of the biblical Jesus. Nevertheless, although believers find the gospel to be strongly attractive, they must also expect it to issue challenges, which they may be reluctant to accept. Jesus sometimes makes claims, which his followers do not find congenial. It is through resistance to these claims that smorgasbord theology arises.

One reason for this kind of theology is that some of Jesus's teachings are regarded as ethically distasteful. Such teachings may include warnings against pride and self-assertion, two qualities which are highly esteemed in some modern western cultures. They may also include his reminders of the dangers of wealth, his condemnation of violence, and his advocacy of a strict sexual morality; and in all these respects his teachings point in directions contrary to fashions, which prevail in modern society. Moreover, he claims from his followers a loyalty which takes precedence over all other loyalties, including allegiance to social group and family,[1] and this claim naturally provokes a great deal of resistance.

Another reason for smorgasbord theology is that some of Jesus's claims are regarded as intellectually distasteful. Many people resist the idea that the human being, Jesus of Nazareth, was uniquely related to God, that he performed miracles, came to save men and women from sin and death, and was raised from the dead. There is even greater hostility to the assertion that God will actually bring history to a close through the agency of Jesus Christ, and perhaps do it by means which are not predictable from the evidence contained in scientific textbooks. Christians, especially those with pretensions to intellectual attainment, do not want to be dubbed 'naive' or 'simplistic' in their thinking. They do not wish to be branded as mental inhabitants of the Dark or Middle Ages, let alone of the world of early Christianity. They are afraid of incurring the scorn of 'modern man', although they find it difficult to describe a typical modern man, and their notion of him is unlikely to fit the majority of the present inhabitants of the earth. The basic cause of this uneasiness is a reluctance to admit the sovereignty of God or to regard him as the creator who has ultimate control of the destinies of his universe. Human intellect is a gift of God which can be used in his service, but if it is to serve him adequately, it needs to recognize that he is not limited by theories contrived by human thought.

Revealed religion discloses truths which are neither expected nor desired. In the process of accustoming themselves to such truths, Christians may try to avoid the challenge of Jesus, resorting to a smorgasbord theology, selecting their preferences and rejecting the rest. Symptomatic of this kind of theology are the other two causes of misinterpretation which have been discussed: the use of words at an insignificant level of generality and the acceptance of rejected options of the gospel. In order to preserve the integrity of Christian interpretation of the Scriptures, it is necessary to be on guard against these tendencies, which make the individual rather than Jesus Christ the ultimate authority.

Since Christianity is not a legalistic religion but a religion of the Spirit, it does not provide a cut-and-dried answer to every theological problem or specific regulations for every conceivable situation in daily life. The biblical Jesus does not exercise his authority by providing a treatise on systematic theology or an exhaustive and comprehensive code of laws. It is as individuals reflect on the acounts of Jesus in the Scriptures that they begin to understand the meaning of his revelation of God and to discern the importance of his teaching and example for the conduct of daily life; but individuals must themselves discover which are the main features of the portrait of Jesus. They have to decide whether the narratives and teaching of the Bible address them by way of challenge or exhortation or warning or promise. They must consider where in a passage of Scripture are the discovery-points for Jesus, God, the self and the other person or creature. A subjective element in Christian interpretation is inevitable; it belongs to the nature of the Christian faith. However, it is only one element in Christian interpretation, and if the interpretation is to be faithful and responsible, it is an element which must always be kept under control and which should always be diminishing.

Over against this subjective element in interpretation is the objective element of the Scriptures themselves. Their contents remain the same. Their accounts of Jesus remain the same. No personal preferences can make any difference to these things. The Scriptures themselves set limits to the area within which serious interpretation can take place. If the plain meaning of the Scriptures is disregarded, or if it is understood at an insignificant level of generality, or if the options rejected by Jesus are accepted, Christian interpretation has ceased to take place. The danger of lapsing into smorgasbord theology is an occupational hazard for anybody who seeks guidance from the study of the Bible, but the very existence of the Scriptures themselves and the very presence there of the accounts of Jesus provide a counterbalance to the subjective element in interpretation.

Another safeguard against smorgasbord theology is the spiritual presence of the biblical Jesus in Christians as they study the Bible. The more they reflect in faith on the accounts of Jesus in the New Testament, the more they are likely to develop an ability to see life as Jesus saw it and to apply the Scriptures to the problems of daily life in ways which are consistent with his teaching and example. Increasing familiarity with the biblical Jesus diminishes the subjective element in a person's attempt to understand the Bible with Jesus as interpreter. When the inner life is nourished by frequent reflection on the biblical Jesus, the Spirit of Jesus Christ truly dwells in a person. In this way, the objective and subjective elements mingle with each other. The biblical Jesus, who is the objective element, influences the judgements and decisions of the inner self, which is the subjective element.

It is of the nature of Christianity that it gives rise to different accounts of the meaning of the gospel. In the New Testament Jesus is seen from a variety of vantage points, through the eyes of several different writers. Christianity is not a religion for robots. It does not programme people to act like automata. It is a religion for free men and women, who freely submit themselves to the authority of Jesus, and who seek to know his will not by memorizing a complex code of regulations but through a growing acquaintance with him. This is how the first Christians learned to know him. It is how the New Testament writers acquired their knowledge of him. The danger of lapsing into a smorgasbord theology always remains. It is a price paid for a religion of the Spirit. There is always the temptation to give the real allegiance to one's self, to one's own likes and dislikes, and to claim the authority of Christ for decisions and judgements, which are alien to the biblical Jesus. It is a danger inherent in the very nature of Christianity, which can be avoided by constant reflection on Jesus as he is depicted in the Bible.

Denial of the Relevance of Jesus's Teaching

Smorgasbord theology is usually accompanied by a denial of the relevance of some central themes of Jesus's teaching for the modern world. One reason given for taking this attitude to his teaching is the great difference between the modern way of life and that of first-century Palestine. That differences exist is obvious. In their modes of transport and their method of disseminating information the two worlds are far removed from each other. The standard of living in modern civilization is such that the middle-class home in the Western world is more comfortable than an ancient palace, but in some respects the passage of many centuries has made little difference to the pattern of human life. The tendency to the unbridled use of violence is as strong now as it was in the days of Jesus. Greed for money and other forms of property is as rampant now as then. Indifference to sexual morality in the modern age rivals that displayed in the ancient world. In these matters Jesus's teaching is as relevant today as it was then. To deny its relevance because of a changed situation is to turn a blind eye to the striking similarities between the two civilizations.

It is also claimed that much of Jesus's teaching is irrelevant because of the differences between modes of thought about the universe in the ancient and in the modern world. Many people now reject the belief that the world was created in six days. Many of them no longer think of the earth as the centre of the universe or of heaven as a place in outer space. Such changes of thought do not diminish the relevance of Jesus's essential teaching. He was not concerned to provide a scientific textbook about the workings of the universe. The basic truths which he communicated do not depend on the literal accuracy of ancient accounts about a six-day creation or the geographical location of heaven. The belief in God as creator need not depend on the acceptance of the precise accuracy of the stories of creation in Genesis. The belief that he has an eternal destiny for men and women can be sustained without the conviction that heaven is a physical place in outer space. Jesus's understanding of God as one who shows a personal love and care for men and women does not depend for its validity on a literal acceptance of every biblical statement about the creation and about heaven. Nor is his ethical teaching undermined by scientific discoveries and theories about the universe.

Sometimes the relevance of Jesus's teaching is denied on the grounds that it is founded on his mistaken assumption that the world was soon to come to an end. It is by no means certain that he made this assumption; but, even if he did, his teaching would still be relevant for today. He himself admitted that he did not know the day or the hour of that final event. It was not of supreme importance to him to be aware of its exact date. But it was of supreme importance to him that men and women should be adequately prepared for it, whenever it should occur. They can be prepared for it by observing the standards set by Jesus about love of neighbour, ministry to the needy, sexual purity, the avoidance of violence, and freedom from obsession with worldly wealth. If these had been matters of indifference, he might well have allowed his disciples to commit adultery, embezzle money, beat up their neighbours, and neglect any kind of assistance to the poor and the infirm. His advocacy of particular styles of conduct as a preparation for the ultimate encounter with God is evidence that these were the styles of conduct of which he approved in everyday life. His standards remain, whether the last day is to occur next week or after a million years.

Yet another reason given for denying the relevance of some of Jesus's teaching is that it envisages an ideal of conduct which is impracticable in the present state of the world. Turning the other cheek, giving money to everyone in need, and abstinence from hatred and from lustful thoughts are sheer impossibilities, it is argued, in the world as it is now constituted. Jesus, it is claimed, teaches an ideal ethic designed for a future kingdom of heaven but not for the present conditions of human existence. This argument completely takes away the sting from some of the most challenging and disturbing aspects of Jesus's teaching. It is ironical that some of the advocates of this argument also give strong support to the dogma of the literal inerrancy of the Scriptures. Yet they bypass some of Jesus's most serious and insistent challenges by the device of treating them as a blueprint for a future Utopia. It is indeed difficult to put all of Jesus's ethical teaching into practice in daily life, and it may not always be appropriate to obey it with exact literalness; but it is not difficult to accept its challenge. Any serious profession of Christian discipleship should include an acceptance of his challenge and a refusal to acquiesce in a way of life which is at variance with his teaching. The basic question is not whether Christians are obeying all Jesus's teaching legalistically, but whether they are paying serious attention to the direction in which he is pointing. In fact he is pointing away from many of the standards accepted by modern society just as he points away from the standards accepted by ancient society.

The tendency to deny the relevance of various aspects of Jesus's teaching is widespread. In one way or another attempts are made to draw the teeth from some of the most challenging and distinctive features of his message. If the biblical Jesus is to be taken seriously, however, an attempt should be made to discover the relevance of everything that he says. There is no easier way of making Jesus conform to our own preconceived ideas than to dismiss aspects of his teaching from consideration, on the grounds that they are not relevant for us today. In this way we can easily fall into the trap of making him say whatever we want and of silencing him, whenever his message displeases us. If he is treated as a genuine authority, we must be ready to look for relevance in his message even when it is not immediately apparent to us. He may in fact be awakening us to important issues which we had not previously noticed. He may be giving challenges to us where we thought that we had no need to be challenged. The consequence of denying the relevance of parts of Jesus's teaching is that in important matters he is not allowed to interpret the Scriptures at all. Or if he is allowed to do so, it is a truncated Jesus who is interpreter, and therefore misinterpretation takes place. A smorgasbord theology is the result. In the name of Jesus an assortment of teaching is conveyed which neglects the directions in which he pointed and gives a distorted impression of the message which he wished to convey.

12
Finding the Way

The Direction in Which Jesus Points

Jesus shows men and women the direction in which they should chart the course of their lives. In allowing him to guide us through life, however, it is not sufficient just to consider negative matters like the options which he rejected. It is important to discover the positive ways in which he sheds light on daily life. The direction in which he points need not be expressed in the form of specific commands uttered by him. Since many of his sayings are concerned with particular situations which arose in his ministry, it is not always appropriate for them to be treated as laws to be obeyed without question in the present day. On the other hand, there needs to be a clear, unmistakable resemblance between Jesus's understanding of God and any Christian understanding of God. There ought also to be a clear, unmistakable resemblance between the style of life commended by him and the style of life advocated in his name. These similarities can be ensured only when attention is paid to the direction in which he points. Although he did not write a systematic theology or give definite rules for every situation in life, his teaching and example provide a clear indication of the way in which he wishes men and women to think of God and the way in which he wishes them to live. He has not bequeathed to his followers a list of articles of faith or a detailed code of law. He points a way through life which has possibilities for variation but which proceeds within discernible limits. The winds of his Spirit do not force men and women into a closely confined channel. They send them across open seas in which there is great freedom of movement; but if men and women accept his authority, although they do not follow precisely the same course as each other, they move in the same direction, a direction which is given to them by him.

The way in which he points can partly be discerned by an examination of the options which he rejected. When he dissociated himself from the viewpoint of the Sadducees, who denied a belief in a future life, he affirmed the very belief which they denied. When he refused the option of starting a violent revolution, he indicated that he wished to achieve his ends by peace and reconciliation. When he rejected an easy attitude to divorce, he showed that he took a stricter position about the matter than most Jews of his day. When he refused to take a purely external attitude to the law, he reinforced his emphasis on the importance of a person's inner thoughts and motives. His refusal to be hostile and exclusive in his treatment of the despised outcasts of society is evidence of his eagerness to befriend them. By rejecting these options, he showed the positive direction in which he wished his followers to move in their thoughts and actions. To each of these options, which he rejects, there corresponds an option which he accepts. It is the accepted option which constitutes the direction in which he is pointing.

There are other directions indicated by Jesus besides those which are the antitheses of rejected options. They are discovered by looking for the beliefs and principles implied by Jesus's teaching and activities. For example, his repeated use of the title 'Father' for God indicates that he understands God as personal, as loving men and women, as caring for them, and as active in them. Once this direction in which Jesus points is understood, it becomes impossible to speak of God merely as a principle of movement or process in history or as an impersonal force of nature. It becomes equally impossible to reduce him to nothing more than a relationship between people, and to regard him only as a synonym for the word 'love', but not as one who actually loves men and women. It is not wrong to speak of God as 'force' or as 'being' or as 'love'. All these ways of speaking about him are consistent with the revelation of him given by Jesus, provided that they are not regarded as exhaustive accounts of his nature. To assume that they give a complete description of him is to set sail on the wrong course. They do not clearly indicate the personal nature of God.

An objection has been raised to the use of the word 'Father' for God, on the grounds that it creates a misleading image of him in the minds of people who have had unhappy relationships with their human fathers. Once it is understood, however, that God is being connected with the ideal of fatherhood and not with the failure of particular men to live up to that ideal, the use of the word to describe him should present no difficulty. Another objection is that 'Father' implies that God is male, whereas in reality he is neither male nor female; but Jesus does not use the word in order to teach that God is masculine; he uses it to show that God combines authority and discipline with love and care in ways which are characteristic of the best in both fatherhood and motherhood. He reveals God as one who takes initiatives towards men and women, responds to them, shows mercy and forgiveness to them, and who in fact has a personal relationship with them. These are the assumptions of Jesus's teaching about God. These are the directions in which he is pointing.

In beliefs about God's purpose for men and women as well as in beliefs about his nature, Jesus shows the direction in which his followers can move. An example of this is to be found in his teaching about the future. His message on this theme is not confined to the assurance that there is life after death. He predicts that history will reach a climax in a final event. Even though he may not have intended all the imagery, which he used in describing this event, to be taken literally, there is no doubt that he taught it would really take place. Any theology, which speaks of the future life merely in terms of a continuing existence immediately after death, neglects the strong emphasis of Jesus on God's intention to bring the whole history of the world to a climax.[1] God's purpose for the future is not just concerned with human beings. His plan of redemption extends to the whole of creation.

Another central theme of Jesus's teaching is that God can give men and women a new kind of life in the present, even before the end of history and before the moment of physical death. He claimed that Jewish expectations about the coming of God's kingdom were already being realized in his ministry. To follow in the direction in which Jesus points is to recognize that God's purposes have rich fulfilment here and now. A theology, which concentrates on the future to the neglect of the present, has diverged from the direction indicated by Jesus as much as a theology which is devoid of any future hope.

Some of Jesus's statements contain important implications about himself. They depict him as uniquely related to God, as both human and divine. The biblical portraits of Jesus show that in a unique way he made it possible for men and women to receive forgiveness of sins and to enter into a new kind of life. His death and resurrection are regarded as integral events in the performance of his redemptive work. The way is left open for the development of different theories of the atonement, which speculate about the precise way in which that work was accomplished; but whatever theory is adopted, a theology, which suggests that these events are not integral to his work, is moving in a direction opposite to that in which he himself is pointing.

The examples which have been considered are concerned with directions in which Jesus points as he interprets both God and himself, but he also interprets us. He shows us the sinfulness of our nature and stresses our dependence on God's mercy. He challenges us to consider the extent of our disobedience to God, and calls on us to repent and to turn to God. He assures us that God can direct the course of our lives. As he reveals to us our present condition, he also tells us about the kind of life which can be lived under God's guidance. He speaks of the two great commandments of love, exhorting us to love God and to love our neighbours. He goes even further than these commandments, and tells us to love our enemies. He commends worship and prayer, emphasizing the need for sincerity in these matters rather than for the meticulous performance of ritual acts. As for the relationship of people to each other, he tells them to practice mercy and forgiveness. He exhorts them to care for people's needs, to show humility, and to avoid self-glorification and pride.[2] He commissions his disciples to bear witness to their faith in word as well as in deed. He authorizes them to tell others of his message about the Kingdom of God.[3] As far as particular issues of conduct are concerned, in addition to his teaching about violence and sex, which has already been discussed, he issues repeated warnings about the dangers of material wealth.[4] He insists on truthfulness of speech, even when a person is not under oath.[5] He stresses the need for inner purity, the absence of anger and the avoidance of lust. He tells his followers to refrain from insulting language and to avoid carping judgements of others.[6] All these themes are among the plainest of the directions provided by Jesus's example and teaching.

There is in some cases ambiguity about the extent to which Jesus's teaching should be taken literally in every instance in which it is applied to the situations of daily life. It is a matter of debate whether his teaching about non-resistance to violence[7] was intended to cover all situations. It is clear that he did not wish his disciples to resist persecution during their missionary work. It is not clear that he intended his words to dissuade people from serving in armies or police forces. However, it is certain that, when he was confronted with the choice between violent revolution and non-resistance, he chose the latter. His teaching and example moved in the direction of peaceful reconciliation. Those who follow in his direction will let him influence their attitude to modern problems. The suggestion that Christians should give support to repressive authoritarian governments, on the one hand, or violent revolutionary movements, on the other, will be brought under the scrutiny of the biblical Jesus. The advocacy of the indiscriminate ownership of handguns will be examined in his light. To take Jesus seriously is to follow in his direction. He did not give a set of rules for every situation, but for the Christian, the direction in which he points is a major factor to be considered in making decisions about conduct in private or in public life.

As for material possessions, Jesus, it is often observed, did not ask all men and women, as he asked the rich young ruler, to sell all their goods and give the proceeds to the poor,[8] but he uttered a stern warning about the danger of worshipping material wealth. He spoke of the almost insuperable difficulty for a rich person to enter the Kingdom of God, a difficulty, which could be overcome only by the grace of God, with whom all things were possible.[9] A serious attempt to follow in the direction given by Jesus must pay attention to this aspect of his teaching. It may be appropriate for Christians to devote some of their energies to making money. But Jesus indicates that the worth of men and women is not to be measured by the extent of their property or the amount of their salaries. The making of money should in no sense be the primary aim in life. It should always be subordinate to the service of God. People cannot serve both God and mammon.[10] There is no doubt about the direction in which Jesus points in this matter.

In dealing with sexual morality and marriage, Jesus puts forward a more rigorous standard than that of the Jewish world in which he was brought up. He showed friendship and understanding to people with a reputation for sexual immorality; but he advocated standards of conduct which exceeded the requirements of the Jewish law. It was not sufficient, he said, to abstain from the outward act of adultery. The adulterous desire was a sin.[11] As for divorce, his line was stricter than that of most Jews of his day. He forbade it, except, according to Matthew's Gospel, on the grounds of adultery.[12] It is possible that he might have treated some marriage breakdowns as exceptions to his general rule, and have sanctioned the divorce of the partners. There is no evidence of any occasion on which he made such an exception, but in view of his love and consideration for individuals, it is conceivable that it might have happened. It is highly likely too that he would have shown understanding of the predicament of the people involved. But even if he might have made exceptions to his rule, the direction in which he points is perfectly clear. Marriage is a lifelong union. When people are joined together in matrimony, they are joined in a union which is to be broken only by death. Modern Western society, however, has reached a stage when an extremely large proportion of marriages end in divorce. The rule given by Jesus is being disregarded to such an extent that the very institution of marriage is in danger of collapse. If modern Christianity is to take the authority of the biblical Jesus seriously, it needs to put a high priority on letting people know what his standards are.

Jesus's teaching and example are relevant to all areas of daily life. Even situations not specifically dealt with by him can be illuminated by him. He does not, for example, give any blue-print for government welfare schemes or health services, but a Christian approach to these matters has to take account of his attitude to poverty and sickness. Christians have a responsibility to see that people are properly fed and clothed, and that the sick are adequately cared for. Although the biblical Jesus does not outline a programme for dealing with these problems, his behaviour throughout his ministry shows that these issues should be of central importance for all who live under his guidance. His teaching and example are also highly relevant to modern discussions of crime, punishment and the prison system. A Christian approach to these questions moves in the direction in which Jesus points, aiming at the rehabilitation of criminals rather than the exacting of retribution from them.[13] Anyone who tries to put Christianity into practice in modern society needs to remember that Jesus cared for the sick, befriended the poor and the disreputable, and encouraged his disciples to follow his example. This is the direction in which he pointed.

In its corporate life the Christian Church receives guidance from him. He does not prescribe a detailed form of church organization. It is not clear from his practice and teaching whether the government of the Church should be papal or episcopal or presbyterian or congregational. Obviously it must have some form of government, and a responsible decision about the matter has to be made in the light of Jesus himself. Organization, however, is not the subject about which he gives the clearest direction to the Church. He left his followers with instructions to serve one another, to preserve unity among themselves and to preach the gospel. He gave them the promise of his continuing presence and the assurance of the gift of the Holy Spirit.[14] He left them with a sacred meal of bread and wine, and the words which he spoke at it provide guidelines for understanding its meaning.[15] According to John's Gospel, his disciples practised baptism during his ministry, and according to Matthew, after his resurrection, he commissioned them to baptize people of all nations.[16] He told his followers that prayer should be earnest and sincere.[17] There is more light shed by the biblical Jesus on matters of worship and community spirit than on the details of church organization.

The teaching and example of Jesus do not give an exhaustive account of Christian doctrine or a complete set of instructions for daily conduct. Many issues are not clearly dealt with by the biblical Jesus. But he gives guidance for confronting all of them. When he is allowed to interpret the Scriptures, his own characteristics are more clearly discerned, and the direction in which he points becomes more apparent.

Areas of Interpretation

Jesus does more than interpret the Bible. He also interprets God, since he is the unique revealer of God. He enables men and women to have a new understanding of God and his purposes. He gives them knowledge of the work, the fruit and the gifts of the Holy Spirit. He provides them with an understanding of himself, of his own unique relationship to his Father, and of the unique work which he performs. His light shines on the Scriptures in order that it may shine on God and on himself.

He is also the interpreter of men and women. He leads them to a clearer knowledge of themselves in their relationship to God and to other people, and indeed to the whole universe. The Scriptures can adequately interpret us, only when we let Jesus interpret the Scriptures. If we try to let them interpret us without light from him, we make ourselves the interpreters and blind ourselves to the illumination which he brings. He is the one who can show us what we are really like, and what we can become.

Through the Bible, Jesus's light shines on the whole of life. He can be the interpreter of other literature as well as the Scriptures, enabling us to read it in his light, and being discovered there by his presence or similarity or contrast. The approach which has been outlined here can be used in reading other books whether they are Christian or not. In any writings which give accounts of human relationships there are points of discovery for the self and for others. Plays, novels and poetry are rich in material where readers may find similarity or contrast between themselves and the characters depicted there. With equal ease it is possible to discover other people in some of the characters. While God and Jesus cannot so easily be found there, it is always possible to consider if the actions and thoughts described in a work of literature are in accordance with God's will and in harmony with the example and teaching of Jesus. To look at literature in this way is not to reject the practice of literary criticism. It is to recognize that, for a Christian believer, everything is to be understood in the light of Jesus.

The Biblical Jesus

The areas in which Jesus acts as interpreter cover the whole of reality. He interprets God and himself. He interprets us and other men and women. He can interpret literature, art, music and history; but it is always the biblical Jesus who is the Christian interpreter, and it as the interpreter of the Bible that he most clearly reveals the nature and will of God, and most distinctively gives his challenges, warnings and assurance to men and women.

It is the biblical Jesus, who calls men and women to take notice of the direction in which he points. One of the tragedies of Christian history is the refusal of large numbers of professing Christians to move in that direction. So-called Christian countries have entered into war as readily and waged it as brutally as non-Christian countries. So-called Christian nations have shown no better a record of family loyalty and sexual morality than non-Christian nations. Professing Christians have displayed as much greed for money and property as non-Christians. They have shown an equal capacity to perpetrate exploitation and injustice. They have displayed as great a tendency to practice racial, national, social and religious discrimination. Nor has the organized Church presented a shining example of the unity and peace, to which Jesus called his disciples. Moreover, the beliefs and hopes of Christians as well as their conduct have often strayed from Jesus. Instead of the God who really loves and cares for men and women, a cold, impersonal deity has become the object of worship. There has been an absence of a firm hope for life beyond death. There has been a loss of conviction about a divine purpose in history. Both Jesus's guidance about conduct and his teaching about God have been neglected. While the name of Jesus has been acknowledged in creeds, hymns and doctrinal statements, the direction in which he points has been disregarded in thought and practice. It is through the teaching and example of Jesus, however, that God's will is made known for the present day, calling us to a life of obedience, offering warnings of divine judgment, but at the same time giving assurance of divine help and mercy.

Because Christianity is a religion of the Spirit, it encourages freedom in thought and action. But that freedom is not unbounded. The Christian gospel has distinctive characteristics. The biblical Jesus points in a clearly discernible direction, even though he does not map out every detail of the way. There is always a temptation to abuse the freedom by claiming the name of Christ for philosophies and styles of living which are in conflict with the teaching and example of Jesus. If attention is given to the direction in which Jesus is pointing, the distinctiveness of the Christian message is preserved. Christianity will always have a place for variety and liberty of interpretation; but if the interpretation is to remain Christian, there are limits within which it will be channelled. An avoidance of rejected options and insignificant generalizations, and an attention to the direction given by Jesus will ensure that these limits are observed.

The ultimate authority, to which Christians have access, is not a Church leader or an ecclesiastical council or a statement of doctrinal standards produced by a conference or synod. It is not the pronouncement of a magnetic preacher or a popular religious writer. Nor is it the opinion of a highly esteemed scholar or theologian. It is not even the Bible itself. The ultimate authority is the biblical Jesus. Without him, Christianity lacks its foundation. It is by him that all Church teachings and confessions are to be measured. All statements on questions of doctrine or conduct are to be judged in his light. All religious experience is to be tested by him. Any claim to the guidance and inspiration of the Holy Spirit must be examined to ascertain if the inspiration and guidance really comes from the Spirit of Jesus Christ. Even the Scriptures themselves are to be seen through his eyes. When he is their interpreter, they can be treated as truly Christian Scriptures, vehicles through which he presents his challenges, warnings and assurances to men and women.

In addition to revealing truth about God and giving guidance for daily life, the biblical Jesus provides opportunity for rich religious experience. It is not the lot of everyone to be caught up into the third heaven as Paul was, or to have a vivid vision of Jesus as Teresa of Avila did;[18] but a genuine religious experience is available to anyone who trusts in the biblical Jesus. To read and hear about his life and teaching, to study the Scriptures with him as interpreter, and to move in the direction in which he points is to experience his presence. When two disciples, who walked with him to Emmaus on the first Easter Day, reflected on their experience, they said that their hearts burned within them as he opened the Scriptures to them.[19] This encounter with Jesus is not reserved for the privileged few. It is available for anyone, who lets him interpret the Scriptures. The encounter may not always be warm or joyful. Experience, religious or otherwise, is not confined to moments of joy or peace or ecstasy. Friends react to each other with hostility, irritation and weariness as well as with happiness and warm affection. The experience of Jesus Christ is not limited to moments of great rejoicing and overwhelming emotions of happiness. When he is encountered through the reading or hearing of the Scriptures, when his light is allowed to shine on its pages, and we begin to move in the direction which he has charted, there is religious experience, whether it is of joy or agony, of peace or conflict, of enraptured wonder or weary indifference. Those who receive him in faith can expect positive as well as negative experience. They can expect that amid doubt and conflict and sometimes even amid weariness the certainties and joys will emerge, the conviction that God loves them and has forgiven them, that God can lead them through the paths of life and has an eternal destiny awaiting them. When Jesus is received in faith, it is more than a written portrait of him that they discover in the Scriptures. It is Jesus himself who meets them there.

To encounter Jesus is not just to experience him. It is to enter within the orbit of his influence. It is to arrive at a place where his Spirit is active. An openness to understand the Bible in his light and an ability to move in the direction charted by him are themselves gifts of the Holy Spirit. The surest place to receive these gifts is where Jesus himself is to be found; and the surest place to find Jesus is in the Scriptures. The more we become acquainted in faith with the biblical Jesus, the more we are likely to recognize the direction in which he is pointing. The closer and more frequent the association which we cultivate with him, the more likely we are to act in the power of his Spirit.

The Bible can be used in a variety of ways. It can be treated as a collection of historical documents or as an anthology of ancient literature; it can be regarded as a collection of proof-texts for one's own theological and philosophical presuppositions; but its distinctively Christian use is to be read and heard in the light of Jesus Christ. When he interprets the Scriptures, God himself is revealed; God's will for men and women is made known. Those, who read or hear the Bible with Jesus as their guide, will not be guilty of according it a superficial lip-service. They will not load it with empty praises. When they speak of its wonder and majesty and riches, their words will be genuine. They will have found in it strength for the present and hope for the future. They will have found there a direction in which to move on the voyage of life. Above all, they will have encountered there Jesus Christ himself.

Notes

Chapter 1

1. The importance of giving attention to the Bible as Scripture is a central theme of Brevard S. Childs, *An Introduction to the Old Testament as Scripture* (London and Philadelphia 1979). The same author also stresses the importance of interpreting the Bible from the viewpoint of faith in *Biblical Theology in Crisis* (Philadelphia 1970). The recognition that there is a need to go beyond biblical criticism is vigorously stated by Watler Wink, *The Bible in Human Transformation* (Philadelphia 1973), and *Transforming Bible Study* (Nashville 1980 and London 1981). Wink, however, takes a different approach to what lies beyond biblical criticism from that which is outlined here.

2. Matt. 5.21–48.

3. Luke 24.27, 32, 44–9.

4. 1 Cor. 1.26.

Chapter 2

1. Accounts of the great variety of reconstructions of the life and teaching of Jesus are to be found in Albert Schweitzer, *The Quest of the Historical Jesus*, E. T., W. Montgomery (London 1910); Harvey K. McArthur, *The Quest through the Centuries: the Search for the Historical Jesus* (Philadelphia 1966); Charles C. Anderson, *Critical Quests of Jesus* (Grand Rapids 1969); John H. Hayes, *Son of God to Superstar* (Nashville 1976).

2. Examples of writers who regard the four gospels as thoroughly reliable are David Smith, *The days of his flesh: the earthly Life of our Lord and Saviour Jesus Christ* (London 1905); E.F. Harrison, *A Short life of Christ* (Grand Rapids 1968); Donald Guthrie, *Jesus the Messiah: an illustrated life of Christ* (London and Grand Rapids 1972).

3. Scholars in this group vary greatly in their views. For example, John W. Bowman, *The Intention of Jesus* (Philadelphia 1943), C.H. Dodd, *The Founder of Christianity* (London 1971; New York 1970), A.M. Hunter, *The Works and Words of Jesus* (rev. edn., London and Philadelphia 1973), T.W. Manson, *The Servant-Messiah: a study of the public ministry of Jesus* (London 1953; Grand Rapids 1977), Vincent Tay-

lor, *The Life and Ministry of Jesus* (London 1955) ascribe a considerable degree of historical reliability to the first three gospels and are prepared to admit that Jesus made some messianic claims for himself, even though he was reluctant to admit publicly that he was the Messiah. They also believe that Mark's Gospel gives a reliable outline of the ministry of Jesus.

On the other hand, Günther Bornkamm, *Jesus of Nazareth*, E.T., Irene and Fraser McLuskey with James M. Robinson (London 1973 and New York 1975) is more sceptical in his view of the historical accuracy of the gospels. He argues that Jesus never claimed to be Messiah and never spoke of himself as the Son of man, but believed that the Son of man was someone else who was yet to come to earth. Rudolf Bultmann, *Jesus and the Word*, E.T., Louise Pettibone Smith and Erminie Huntress Lantero (New York 1934), is more sceptical than Bornkamm and is not prepared in any way to reconstruct the life of Jesus, although he concludes that certain teachings ascribed to Jesus are historically reliable. He does not think, however, that Jesus had any messianic consciousness.

4. S.G.F. Brandon, *Jesus and the Zealots: a study of the political factor in primitive Christianity* (Manchester 1967); Robert Eisler, *The Messiah Jesus and John the Baptist according to Flavius Josephus' recently discovered 'Capture of Jerusalem' and other Jewish and Christian sources*, Eng. edn A. H. Krappe (New York 1931); H.S. Reimarus, *Reimarus: Fragments*, ed. C.H. Talbert, E.T., Ralph S. Fraser (Philadelphia 1970).

5. Hugh J. Schonfield, *The Passover Plot* (London 1965).

6. William E. Phipps, *Was Jesus married?the distortion of sexuality in the Christian tradition* (New York 1970).

7. Morton Smith, *Clement of Alexandria and a secret gospel of Mark* (Cambridge, Mass. 1973). In another work on the same subject, *The secret gospel: the discovery and interpretation of the secret gospel according to Mark* (New York 1973), pp. 113–14, Smith suggests the possibility that the secret society founded by Jesus might have practised physical union in which Jesus himself participated.

8. John M. Allegro, *The sacred mushroom and the cross: a study of the nature and origin of Christianity within the fertility cults of the Ancient Near East* (London 1970); Arthur Drews, *The Christ myth*, E.T., C. Delisle Burns (Chicago 1911); John M. Robertson, *Christianity and mythology*, 2nd edn. (London 1912); G. A. Wells, *The Jesus of the early Christians: a study in Christian origins* (London 1971); *Did Jesus Exist?* (London 1975).

9. Matt. 7.12; cf. Luke 6.31.

10. For an account of the variety of viewpoints see W.G. Kümmel, in P. Feine, J. Behm and W.G. Kümmel, *Introduction to the New Testament*, E.T. A.J. Mattill, Jr. (Nashville and New York 1966), pp. 33–60.

11. For a discussion of the historical reliability of John's Gospel see C.H. Dodd, *Historical tradition in the Fourth Gospel* (Cambridge 1963); Raymond E. Brown, *The Gospel according to John*, I. (Garden City, New York 1966).

12. For an examination of these categories see Norman Perrin, *The New Testament: an introduction* (New York 1974), pp. 281–2; ibid. *Rediscovering the teaching of Jesus* (London 1967), pp. 39–47.

13. Paul Tillich, *Systematic Theology*, II (London 1957), pp. 130–5, argues that the assertion that Jesus is the Christ is based on the picture of Jesus given by the first three gospels. The position taken here agrees with Tillich's insistence that it is the biblical witness rather than historical research, which provides the basis for the assertion that Jesus is the Christ; but the argument in these pages differs from Tillich in claiming that the basis for Christian faith is to be found in the portraits of Jesus in all four gospels, together with the sketches of him which can be found in other parts of the New Testament. Another difference is that the approach to the biblical Jesus advocated here, puts a great deal more emphasis in practice than does Tillich on the teaching and example of Jesus; nor does it follow Tillich's theory of the resurrection and the return of Christ, which 'deliteralizes' these events to such an extent that it ceases to be clear how far he is really relying on the biblical portraits of Jesus (Tillich, *Systematic Theology*, II, 121–2, 140, 183–90). C.H. Dodd, *The Founder of Christianity*, pp. 47–8, stresses the importance of the total picture of Jesus given in the gospels, and claims that the gospels give a picture of the kind of thing that Jesus did and the kind of attitude and relations which he had. The theme of the gospels as pictures is central to Wayne G. Rollins, *The Gospels, Portraits of Christ* (Philadelphia 1963).

14. In the late nineteenth century Martin Kähler, *The so-called historical Jesus and the historic biblical Christ*, E.T. Carl E. Braaten (Philadelphia 1964), claimed that the Christian faith was founded on Jesus Christ as proclaimed by the biblical writers rather than on the results of the quest for the historical Jesus. His point was a valid one; and in spite of repeated attempts to discover the historical Jesus by critical methods of investigation, his point continues to be true; but although Kähler uses the term 'biblical Christ', it can be seriously misunderstood in the light of the way in which other people have used it. For that reason 'biblical Jesus' is the term which has been preferred here.

Chapter 3

1. Mark 4.35–41; 6.45–52, 30–44; 8.1–10; 1.40–5; 2.1–12; 7.31–7; 9.14–29; 5.21–43; 3.1–6; 1.21–8; 5.1–20; 8.22–6; 10.46–52.

2. See Joachim Rohde, *Rediscovering the Teaching of the Evangelists,* E.T. Dorothea M. Barton (London and Philadelphia 1968); ed. James L. Mays, *Interpreting the Gospels* (Philadelphia 1981).

3. Matt. 11.27; 16.16; 24.36; 28.19; Mark 1.1; 13.32; Luke 1.32, 35; 10.22; Acts 9.20; 13.33; Matt. 3.17; 17.5; Mark 1.11; 9.7; Luke 3.22; 9.35.

4. Matt. 28.1–20; Mark 16.1–8; Luke 24.1–53; Acts 1.1–12. The manuscript evidence suggests that Mark 16.9–20 was not part of the original gospel but was inserted later because of the absence of any accounts of resurrection appearances in the surviving manuscripts of the gospel.

5. Matt. 1.18–25; Luke 1.26–2.20.

6. Matt. 9.1–8; Mark 2.1–12; Luke 5.17–26; 7.36–50.

7. Matt. 8.23–7; Mark 4.36–41; Luke 8.22–5. The response of the disciples and the people to the miracle implies a recognition of Jesus's divinity. Compare Ps. 65.7; 107.28 –30.

8. Matt. 11.27; Luke 10.22.

9. Matt. 17.5; Mark 9.7; Luke 9.35.

10. Matt. 13.11; Mark 4.11; Luke 8.10.

11. Matt. 9.1 –8; Mark 2.1 –12; Luke 5.17–26; 7.36–50. The same Greek word *sozein* ('to save' or 'to make well') is used of both forgiveness and ·physical healing. See Luke 7.50; 8.48.

12. Matt. 20.28; 26.28; Mark 10.45; 14.24.

13. Luke 22.20.

14. Luke 22.37; Acts 8.32–5; 20.28.

15. Luke 9.51; 24.44–9; Acts 2.1–36.

16. Matt. 10.22; 16.25; Mark 8.35; 13.13; Luke 18.7–8; 21.27; Acts 3.19–21.

17. Matt. 16.21; 26.39; Mark 8.31; 14.36; Luke 9.51; 22.42.

18. Matt. 15.1–20; 23.1–36; Mark 7.1–23; 12.38–40; Luke 11.37–44.

19. Matt. 9.9–13; Mark 2.13–17; Luke 5.27–32; 14.1–11; 15.1–32. .

20. Matt. 9.36; 14.14; 15.32; 20.34; Mark 1.41; 6.34; 8.2; 10.21; Luke 7.13.

21. Matt. 5.17; 10.32–3; 11.2–19; 25–30; Mark 1.27; 2.10,17,28; 10.45; 14.61–2; Luke 5.24,32; 6.5; 10.22.

22. Matt. 8.20; Luke 9.58.

23. Matt. 9.9–17; Mark 2.13–22; Luke 5.27–39; 7.36–50; 15.1–2.

24. Matt. 4.1–11; Mark 1.12–13; Luke 4.1–13; cf. Matt. 16.23; Mark 8.33.

25. Matt. 26.38–9; Mark 14.34–6; Luke 22.41–2.

26. Matt. 7.29; Mark 1.22, 27; Luke 4.36.

27. E.g. Matt. 11.27; 17.12; 24.36; Mark 9.31; 10.45; 13.32; 14.61–2; Luke 10.22; 22.22.

28. Matt. 16.20; Mark 8.30; Luke 9.21.

29. E.g. Matt. 16.21; Mark 8.31; Luke 9.22.

30. E.g. Matt. 6.9; 11.25–6; Mark 8.38; 14.36; Luke 10.21; 11.2; 23.46.

31. Matt. 4.17; 12.28; 13.36–43,47–50; 18.10–14; 24.29–25.46; Mark 1.15; 2.5,17; 8.38; 13.1–37; Luke 11.20; 15.1–32; 16.19–31; 17.20–37; 19.11–27; 21.5–36.

32. Matt. 22.34–40; Mark 12.28–34; Luke 10.25–8.

33. Matt. 16.24–7; 19.16–30; 20.20–8; Mark 8.34–8; 10.17–31; 35–45; Luke 9.23–6; 18.18–30; 22.24–7.

34. Matt. 5.31–2, 38–42; 6.19–34; 19.9,23–6; 26.52; Mark 10.11–12,23–7; 14.43–53; Luke 6.27–30; 12.16–21; 16.13,18–31; 18.24–7; 22.49–51.

35. Matt. 5.21–30; 6.1–6,16–18; 15.10–20; Mark 7.14–23; Luke 6.45; Matt. 13.24–30,36–43,47–50; 22.23–33; 24.29–25.46; Mark 8.38; 12.18–27; 13.24–37; Luke 20.27–40; 21.25–36.

36. Matt. 6.5–15; 7.7–11; 26.26–9; Mark 11.24–5;14.22–5; Luke 11.1–13; 18.1–8; 22.14–20.

37. Matt. 12.28; Luke 11.20.

38. Mark 1.16–20; 2.13–14.

39. Matt. 5.31–2; 19.9.

40. Mark 10.11–12; Luke 16.18.

41. Matt. 26.26–9; Mark 14.22–5; Luke 22.14–20.

42. Matt. 20.26–8; Mark 10.43–5; Luke 22.26 –7; Matt. 16.24; Mark 8.34; Luke 9.23.

43. Matt. 10.25; cf. Luke 6.40.

44. Matt. 5.5; 11.29 (AV); cf. 21.5 (AV).

45. Luke 23.34,46; Acts 7.59–60.

46. Luke 9.51,53; 13.33; 17.11; 19.11; Acts 20.16,22; 21.12–13,15.

47. Matt. 28.1–20; Mark 16.1–8; Luke 24.1–53; Acts 2.32; 10.40–1; 13.32–3.

48. Matt. 22.41–6; Mark 12.35–7; Luke 20.41–4; Acts 2.34–6.

49. Luke 24.49; Acts 2.4,33; 4.8,31; 13.2; 15.28.

50. Mark 1.8; 13.11.

51. Matt. 3.11; 10.20; 18.20; 28.20.

52. Matt. 13.36–43,47–50; 24.29–31; 25.31–46; Mark 13.24–37; Luke 21.25–36; Acts 10.42.

53. John 4.25–6; 5.19–29.

54. John 8.58.

55. John 1.1–14.

56. John 6.35, 41, 48, 51; 8.12, 58; 10.7, 9, 11, 14; 11.25; 14.6; 15.1, 5; cf. Exod. 3.14; Isa. 41.4; 43.25.

57. John 20.28.

58. John 1.18.

59. John 14.9.

60. John 12.49.

61. John 3.17; 4.42.

62. John 1.29; 10.11.

63. John 3.16–21.

64. John 6.1–14; 5.1–9; 9.1–41; 11.1–44.

65. John 6.35, 41, 48, 51.

66. John 9.5.

67. John 11.25–6; 5.25–9; 6.40, 44, 54.

68. John 12.27–8.

69. John 7.10–52.

70. John 4.1–42. Another passage, about Jesus's merciful attitude to an adulteress, occurs in John 7.53–8.11. While this probably records an

incident which actually happened, the manuscript evidence shows that it is unlikely to have been part of the original text of John's Gospel.

71. John 2.1–11.

72. John 6.15; 12.27–8.

73. Ernest Käsemann, *The Testament of Jesus: a study of the Gospel of John in the light of chapter 17,* E.T., Gerhard Krodel (London 1968), pp. 26,66,70.

74. John 1.14.

75. John 4.6; 12.27; 13.21; 19.28.

76. E.g. John 1.51; 3.13–14; 5.19–29.

77. John 4.25–6.

78. John 8.58; cf. also the numerous 'I am' sayings; see note 56.

79. John 10.30; 17.22.

80. John 6.40,44,54.

81. John 13.34; 15.12.

82. John 14.15.

83. John 14.26.

84. John 18.1–11.

85. John 6.47–51.

86. Matt. 6.19–21; cf. Matt. 19.21; Mark 10.21; Luke 12.21; 18.22.

87. John 4.16–18.

88. John 13.34; 15.12.

89. John 3.16.

90. John 10.16; 17.20–6.

91. John 14.13–14; 4.23–4; 6.52–9; cf. Matt. 6.5–6.

92. John 13.14–15.

93. John 15.4.

94. John 1.4; 11.25; 14.6.

95. John 20.1–21.25.

96. John 15.26; 16.7; 20.22; 15.4; 17.20–6.

97. John 5.25–9; 6.40, 44, 54.

98. Differences of the sequence of events include the placing of the cleansing at the temple at the beginning of Jesus's ministry instead of the end (Matt. 21.12–17; Mark 11.11, 15–19; Luke 19.45–8; John 2.13–17), the anointing of Jesus at Bethany which is placed before his entry into Jerusalem by John but afterwards by Matthew and Mark (Matt. 26.6–13; Mark 14.3–9; John 12.1–8). As for the exact dates, John dates the Last Supper to the night before the passover sacrifice and dates the crucifixion to the time of the sacrifice (John 13.1; 19.14, 31), while the other gospels date these events a day later (Matt. 26.17; Mark 14.12; Luke 22.7).

Chapter 4

1. Phil. 2.5–11; Col. 1.15–17; 1 Cor. 10.1–5; 2 Cor. 8.9.

2. E.g. Rom. 1.1–7; 1 Cor. 1.3; 8.6; Gal. 1.3, 16.

3. Phil. 2.5–6.

4. 1 Cor. 15.28.

5. Gal. 1.12.

6. Rom. 5.8.

7. 2 Cor. 4.6.

8. Eph. 1.9.

9. Col. 2.3.

10. Phil. 3.20; Eph. 5.23.

11. Rom. 3.24; Gal. 2.15–21; cf. Eph. 2.5,8.

12. 1 Cor. 3.10–15.

13. Cf. Rudolf Bultmann, *Theology of the New Testament,* I, E.T. Kendrick Grobel (New York 1951) pp. 293–4.

14. Phil. 2.5–11.

15. 2 Cor. 10.1.

16. 1 Cor. 11.23–6; 7.10–11.

17. Rom. 12.9–21; 13.8–10; Gal. 5.13–15.

18. Rom. 12.3; Phil. 2.1–4.

19. 2 Cor. 8.8–15; cf. Phil. 4.10–13.

20. 1 Cor. 7.8–12.

21. Phil. 2.5–11.

22. Eph. 5.25–7.

23. Rom. 15.1–2, 7–9.

24. Rom. 6.1–14; 2 Cor. 1.5; 13.1–4; Phil. 3.10–11; Col. 2.12–14; 3.1.

25. 1 Cor. 15.3–4.

26. Rom. 8.34; Eph. 1.20; Col. 3.1.

27. Rom. 8.10; 2 Cor. 5.17; 12.2; Gal. 2.20; Col. 1.17.

28. Rom. 12.3–8; 1 Cor. 12.1–14.40; Eph. 4.11–14.

29. Gal. 5.22–3.

30. Rom. 8.9–11; Gal. 5.16,25.

31. 2 Cor. 5.10; Phil. 3.20–1; Col. 3.4; 1 Thess. 4.13–18; 2 Thess. 1.5–2.12.

32. 2 Cor. 1.22; 5.5; Eph. 1.13–14; cf. Rom. 8.23.

33. The authorship of the Pastoral Epistles (1 and 2 Timothy and Titus) is widely disputed. While the reasons for doubting Pauline authorship are stronger in this case than with any other letter, except that to the Hebrews, it is conceivable that the differences of style between these and the other letters may be accounted for by Paul's use of a secretary to write to Timothy and Titus. In any case, these letters support the main outlines of the portrait of Jesus which have been traced in the other letters. They affirm his unique relationship to God (1 Tim. 2.5; Tit. 2.13), his work as a revealer (2 Tim. 1.10), saviour (1 Tim. 1.15; 2 Tim. 1.10; Tit. 3.6), teacher (1 Tim. 6.3) and example (1 Tim. 1.16; 6.13), and his identity with the risen and coming Christ (1 Tim. 6.14; 2 Tim. 2.8).

34. Heb. 1.1–4.

35. Heb. 1.2.

36. Heb. 1.3; 5.9; 9.28.

37. Heb. 5.7; 12.2.

38. Heb. 2.18; 4.15; 5.8.

39. Heb. 12.2.

40. Heb. 13.12–14.

41. Heb. 1.3; 2.9; 4.14; 12.2.

42. Heb. 7.25; 8.1–2; 9.24.

43. Heb. 9.28.

44. Heb. 13.1–5.

45. Jas. 1.1; 2.1; 1 Pet. 1.3; 2 Pet. 1.2, 11; 2.20; 3.18; 1 John 1.3,7; 4.15; 5.5,20; 2 John 3; Rev. 2.18; 17.14; 19.16; 22.20,21. The Letters of John certainly come from the same school of thought as John's Gospel, and may well have been written by the same author.

46. 1 John 1.1–4; Rev. 1.1; 6.1.

47. Jas. 1.12 (future); 1 Pet. 1.3 (present and future), 5 (future), 18 (present); 2.2 (future), 10 (present) 3.21 (present and future); 2 Pet. 1.11 (future); 1 John 1.7; 4.9–10; 5.12 (present); 3.2–3 (future); Jude 17–25 (future); Rev. future throughout, but 1.5–6; 5.9–10 refer to the present.

48. 1 Pet. 2.22–3; Rev. 1.5.

49. 1 Pet. 2.21.

50. 1 Pet. 1.3,7,11,13; 2 Pet. 1.1,11; 3.18; 1 John 1.3; 5.20; 2 John 3,7; Jude 1,4,21; Rev. 1.5–7; 5.6–12.

51. Jas. 1.1; 2.1; 5.8.

52. Love of neighbour is referred to in Jas. 2.8. Cf. 1 Pet. 1.22; 2 Pet. 1.7; 1 John 2.10; 3.11; 4.7,12,20–1; 2 John 5. The danger of riches is mentioned in Jas. 5.1–6; 1 Pet. 5.2; 2 Pet. 2.14–16; Rev. 3.15–18. The avoidance of sexual immorality is alluded to in 1 Pet. 3.1–2; 2 Pet. 2.1–10; 1 John 2.16; Jude 4; Rev. 2.14,20. Humility is mentioned in Jas. 4.6–10; 1 Pet. 5.5–6. Pride is denounced in Jas. 4.16; 1 Pet. 5.5; 1 John 2.16. Endurance is commended in Jas. 1.3,12; 5.10–11; 1 Pet. 2.19–20; 2 Pet. 1.6; Rev. 2.1–7,19; 3.10.

53. Examples of this kind of apocryphal gospel are the Book of James, the Infancy Gospel of Thomas, and the Gospel of Pseudo-Matthew. For the texts of apocryphal gospels see Edgar Hennecke, *New Testament Apocrypha*, ed. Wilhelm Schneemelcher; E.T. ed. R. McL. Wilson, I (London and Philadelphia 1963).

54. Gospel of Peter 4.10; 5.19. Another gospel which concentrates on the passion is the Gospel of Nicodemus, or Acts of Pilate.

55. Coptic Gospel of Thomas, 114.

56. See Bertil Gärtner, *The Theology of the Gospel of Thomas*, E.T. Eric J. Sharpe (London 1961); H.E.W. Turner and Hugh Montefiore, *Thomas and the Evangelists* (London 1962), pp. 79–116. The texts of various Gnostic writings, including the Gospel of Truth and the Gospels of Mary, Philip, and Thomas, are translated in James M. Robinson (ed.), *The Nag-Hammadi Library* (San Francisco 1977).

57. John 3.3.

58. John 8.12 (cf. 9.5); 6.35,41,48,51.

59. 2 Cor. 12.1–5.

Chapter 5

1. Matt. 5.21–48.

2. Gal. 3.23–4.7; 4.21–5.1.

3. Matt. 5.22.

4. Matt. 16.23; 17.18; Mark 1.25; 8.33; 9.25; Luke 4.35; 9.42.

5. Mark 3.5.

6. Matt. 23.27–36.

7. Matt. 21.12–17; Mark 11.15–19; Luke 19.45–8; John 2.13–17.

8. Matt. 5.22; the additional words are found in the AV and are in most of the later manuscripts, but not in some of the oldest and most reliable manuscripts.

9. Matt. 5.38–48; Luke 6.27–31; Matt. 21.12–17; Mark 11.11, 15–19; Luke 19.45–8; John 2.13–17.

10. Matt. 4.8–10; 26.51–4; Mark 14.48–9; Luke 4.5–8; 22.47–51; John 6.15; 18.10–11.

11. Matt. 5.17.

12. Matt. 5.38–48.

13. The statements in Matt. 5.18–19 have caused a great deal of difficulty, since, according to one interpretation, they could mean that Jesus expected his followers to obey every detail of the law. Such a view would be contrary to the plain teaching of much of the Sermon on the Mount, in which Jesus gives a new interpretation of the law. If Matt. 5.18–19 is not to be written off as inconsistent with the rest of Jesus's teaching, then the statement that not an iota or a dot will pass from the law means that God's law still remains God's law, and is fulfilled in Christ, but it does not mean that God's law, as given to the Israelites, continues to be binding in every detail. The reference to those who break the least of the commandments will refer to the commandments of Jesus in the Sermon on the Mount, not to the commandments of the Mosaic Law. It will agree with the conclusion of the Sermon on the Mount which enjoins obedience to God's will as revealed through the words of Jesus (Matt. 7.21–7).

14. Matt. 5.5; 11.29; 21.5. The same Greek word *praus* is used in all these verses, but RSV uses three different words 'meek', 'gentle', and 'humble', to translate it.

15. 1 Cor. 6.9; 11.2–16.

16. 1 Cor. 14.34; Rom. 13.8; Gal. 5.14.

17. Col. 3.22–5; Eph. 6.5–8; Rom. 12.3.

18. 1 Cor. 11.2–16.

19. Gal. 3.28.

20. Cf. Matt. 9.9–13; 11.4–6; Mark 1.40–5; 2.13–17; Luke 5.27–32; 7.22–3, 36–50; 14.12–14; 15.1–2.

21. Matt. 15.19; Mark 7.21; 1 Cor. 6.9.

22. Rom. 12.3; 13.8–10; Gal. 5.13–15.

23. Rom. 12.4–5; 1 Cor. 12.12, 27; Eph. 1.22–3; Col. 1.18.

24. 1 Cor. 12.4–31; 14.1–40; Rom. 12.6; Gal. 5.22–3; 2 Cor. 5.17; Rom. 6.4; Gal. 2.20.

25. Rom. 3.21–31; Gal. 2.15–21.

26. Luke 18.9–14.

27. Matt. 9.1–8; Mark 1.15; 2.1–12; Luke 5.17–26; 7.36–50; 15.1–32.

28. John 1.17; 3.16.

29. Jas. 2.24; Rom. 3.28.

30. Jas. 1.1; 2.1; 1.17–18.

31. Jas. 5.1–6; 4.11–12; 5.12.

32. Jas. 2.8.

33. Matt. 7.21–7; Luke 6.46–9.

34. Jas. 2.1–7; 3.1–5.

35. Mark 13.33; Acts 1.7; Mark 13.32; cf. Matt. 24.36,42–4; 25.13; Luke 21.34–6.

36. Rev. 11.7; 13.1–18; 14.9; 17.7–18; 19.17–21.

37. Rev. 14.9–11; 20.11–15; 21.8.

38. Rev. 6.1–17; 8.1–9.21; 16.1–21.

39. Rev. 1.12–20; 6.1–17; 8.1; 22.16.

Chapter 6

1. Gen. 9.20–7; 12.10–20; 25.29–34; 27.1–40; 2 Sam. 11.1–12.25.

2. Gen. 6.5–7.24; Exod. 11.1–12.36; 2 Kings 23.26–7; Isa. 7.20; 8.5–8.

3. Deut. 20.10–18; Num. 31.1–41; Josh. 6.15–25; 1 Sam. 15.1–35.

4. Ps. 137.8–9. Other imprecatory psalms include Psalms 58; 69; 79. A good discussion of Old Testament passages which conflict with the standards of Jesus is found in Frederick W. Farrar, *The Bible: its meaning and supremacy* (London, New York, and Bombay 1897), pp. 78–91.

5. Theodoret, *Quaest. in Jos.* 7; *Quaest. in Num.* 48; *Quaest. in Lib. Prim. Reg.,* 34; *Quaest. in Ps. 136* (PG LXXX 470, 399, 564, 1930). Theodoret, like other early Christian writers, numbers the psalms differently from the Hebrew Bible and others based on it. Ps. 137 in the Hebrew Bible is numbered 136 by these early Christians, in agreement with the LXX.

6. Matt. 5.38–41.

7. Origen, *in Lib. Jesu Nave Hom.,* 6.3–7.7; *in Num. Hom.,* 25.4–6, *PG* XII 854–63, 767–70.

8. Bede, *in Sam. prophetam allegorica expos.* 2.11, *PL* XCI 601–2.

9. Augustine, *Enarr. in Ps. 136,* 21, *PL* XXXVII 1773–4.

10. John Chrysostom, *Expos. in Ps. 136,* 2, *PG* LV 407.

11. Psalm 137 was one of the psalms omitted by John Wesley from his Sunday Service book for American Methodists as 'being highly improper for the mouths of a Christian congregation' (*The Works of John Wesley,* London 1872, repr. Grand Rapids n.d., XIV, 304). His brother Charles, however, gave a similar interpretation of the psalm to that of Augustine (*The Poetical Works of John and Charles Wesley,* London 1870, VIII, 252–4).

12. Gen. 12.1–9; Exod. 5.1–14.31; 2 Sam. 12.1 –14; 1 Kings 18.1–19.18; Jer. 11.18–12.6; 15.10–21; 20.1–18; 26.1–24; 36.1–45.5.

Chapter 7

1. Matt. 22.2; Luke 19.12; Matt. 13.24,37.

2. E.g. Joachim Jeremias, *Parables of Jesus,* E.T., S.H. Hooke, revised ed. (London and New York 1971).

3. See Matthew Black, 'The Parables as allegory', *Bulletin of the John Rylands Library,* XLII (1960), pp. 273–87.

4. Rev. 5.5–6; 19.11–16.

5. 1 Cor. 7.8–16.

6. Matt. 7.29; Mark 1.22; Luke 4.32; John 6.63.

7. John 1.18.

8. Matt. 11.27; cf. Luke 10.22.

9. Matt. 9.6; 12.8; 16.27; Mark 2.10,28; 8.38; Luke 5.24; 6.5; 9.26; John 6.40,44,54.

10. Mark 4.41; cf. Matt. 8.27; Luke 8.25; Ps. 65.7; 107.28–9.

1¹. Col. 1.16; Heb. 1.2.

12. John 1.3–14.

13. Acts 2.1–4.

14. Rom. 8.9–11.

15. John 16.13.

16. Matt. 22.2.

17. Matt. 21.33–46; Mark 12.1–12; Luke 20.9–19.

18. Matt. 22.34–40; Mark 12.28–34; Luke 10.25–8; cf. Deut. 6.5; Lev. 19.18.

19. Matt. 26.69–75; Mark 14.66–72; Luke 22.54–62; John 18.15–27; Matt. 19.16–22; Mark 10.17–22; Luke 18.18–23.

20. Luke 10.38–42; John 13.1–20.

21. Luke 12.13–21.

22. Luke 18.1–8.

23. 1 Cor. 1–3; 5–7; 11.17–34; 12; 14.

24. Matt. 8.5–13; Luke 7.1–10.

25. Matt. 26.6–13; Mark 14.3–9; John 12.1–8; cf. Luke 7.36–50.

26. Matt. 25.1–13.

27. Matt. 13.45–6.

28. For the emphasis on boldness see Acts 4.13, 31; 9.27, 29; 14.3; 18.26; 19.8; 28.31.

29. Matt. 25.14–30; cf. Luke 19.12–27.

30. Acts 4.13, 31.

31. Matt. 19.22; Mark 10.22; Luke 18.23.

32. Luke 12.32.

33. 1 Cor. 12.12, 27; Rom. 12.4–5; Eph. 1.22–3; Col. 1.18.

34. 1 Pet. 2.9; cf. 1 Pet. 2.5.

35. Acts 17.21, 32–4.

36. 1 Pet. 5.13; Rev. 17.5; 18.2, 21.

37. Acts 19.23–41.

38. Matt. 11.20–4; Luke 9.51–6; 10.13–15.

39. See note 18.

40. Matt. 7.12; cf. Luke 6.31.

41. Matt. 5.22, 32; 7.1; 19.9; Mark 10.11–12; Luke 6.37; 16.18.

42. Luke 10.29–37.

43. 1 Cor. 8.1–13; 10.14–11.1.

44. Acts 19.23–41.

45. Matt. 6.26–30; 10.29; Luke 12.6, 24–8.

46. Rom. 8.18–25; Eph. 1.9–10; Col. 1.19–20.

47. Matt. 22.1–10.

48. Luke 10.29–37.

49. Luke 15.11–32.

50. Ambrose, *Expos. in Luc.* 7. 71–84, *PL* XV 1805–8; Augustine, *Quaest. Evang.* 2.19, *PL* XXXV 1340–1; cf. Origen in *Luc. Hom.* 34, *PG* XIII 1886–8.

Chapter 8

1. Augustine, *in Ep. Joann. ad Parthos* 2.2, *PL* XXXV 1843.

2. Martin Luther, *D. Martin Luthers Werke,* Kritische Gesamtausgabe XI (Weimar 1900), 223.

3. Deut. 18.18–20.

4. Isa. 9.6.

5. Isa. 11.1.

6. Isa. 7.14; cf. Matt. 1.22–3.

7. Ps. 2.1–2.

8. Ps. 2.7.

9. Ps. 110.1.

10. Although he argues that Ps. 110 refers only to Christ, Calvin claims that Psalm 2 refers to both David and Christ (John Calvin, *Commentary on the Book of Psalms,* E.T. James Anderson, Grand Rapids 1946), I,9–27; IV, 295–310.

11. Jer. 31.31–4; cf. 1 Cor. 11.25; 2 Cor. 3.5–6; Heb. 8.1–13; 9.15.

12. Isa. 65.17; 66.22; cf. 2 Pet. 3.13; Rev. 21.1–22.5.

13. Isa. 42.1–4; 49.1–6; 50.4–11; 52.13–53.12.

14. E.g. Matt. 8.17; 12.17–21; Luke 22.37; Acts 8.32–5; 1 Pet. 2.21–5.

15. Matt. 17.10–13; Mark 9.11–13; Luke 9.52–6 (where a contrast is implied with Elijah's behaviour in 2 Kings 1.1–12); Acts 1.1–2.4 (where a resemblance is probably implied to Elijah's ascension and the gift of his Spirit to Elisha in 2 Kings 2.1–15); Acts 3.20–1 (where Jesus appears to be fulfilling the prophecies of Mal. 4.5–6 and Ecclus. 48.10); Rev. 11.5–7 (cf. 1 Kings 18.1–46; 2 Kings 1.1–12).

16. Gen. 1.27; 2 Cor. 4.4; Col. 1.15.

17. E.g. Gen. 32.28; Isa. 41.8. In John 15.1 the words, 'I am the true vine' imply that Jesus embodies Israel.

18. Cf. Heb. 9.15ff.

19. E.g. Matt. 2.6; Luke 1.32–3; John 1.49.

20. 2 Kings 2.1–15; Acts 1.1–12; 2.1–4.

21. Matt. 5.21–48.

22. John 1.17; 6.31–4; 3.14–15.

23. Luke 9.51–6; cf. 2 Kings 1.1–16.

24. Acts 2.24–32.

25. John 4.7–15.

26. Rom. 5.15–21; 1 Cor. 15.45.

27. Heb. 9.11–14.

28. Matt. 26.28; Mark 14.24. In some texts of Luke 22.20 the same idea is present.

29. John 1.29; 19.14,31.

30. 1 Cor. 5.7; 1 Pet. 1.18–19; Rev. 1.5–6; 5.12; Acts 20.28.

31. Heb. 7.23–8; 9.6–10.25.

32. Rom. 5.14.

33. Origen, *in lib. Jesu Nave Hom.* 3.4–5; 6.3–7.7, *PG* XII 839–42; 854–63.

34. Origen, *in Lib. Jud. Hom.* 8.1, *PG* XII 982. See Judges 8.10.

35. See pp. 58–60.

36. E.T., M. Simon, *Midrash Rabbah; Song of Songs* (London 1939).

37. Origen, *in Cant.* 1 (1.1), *PG* XIII 83.

38. *Ibid.* 1 (1.4), *PG* XIII 98. See Song of Sol. 1.4.

39. Gen. 37.5–11; 40.1–41.36; Dan. 2.1–45; 4.1–27; 7.1–8.26.

40. Matt. 13.1–30, 36–43; Mark 4.1–20; Luke 8.4–15.

41. Rev. 6.1–8; 12.1–13.18; 17.1–18.

42. John 1.3; Col. 1.16–17; Heb. 1.2.

43. 1 Cor. 10.4; John 12.37–41.

44. John and Charles Wesley, *Poetical Works* XI (London 1871), p. 309.

Chapter 9

1. Isa. 9.2.

2. Isa. 9.6.

3. Isa. 53.5,12.

4. Isa. 65.17; 66.22.

5. Jer. 31.31–4.

6. Deut. 6.4–5; Lev. 19.18.

7. Exod. 21.23–4; Lev. 24.19 –20; Deut. 19.21.

8. Rom. 12.1; Heb. 13.15–16.

9. 1 Sam. 17.1–54; 2 Sam. 11.1–12.25.

10. E.g. Josh. 4.1–8.35.

11. Judges 4.4–24; 5.24–7.

12. Gen. 25.29–34; 27.1–40.

13. Gen. 12.10–20.

14. Exod. 8.19; 9.34, etc.; Dan. 3.1–30.

15. Gen. 16.1–6; 21.1–7.

16. Isa. 6.1–13; Ezek. 1.1–28.

17. Matt. 6.26–9; 10.29; Luke 12.6,24–7.

18. 1 Sam. 17.1–58. There have been various interpretations of Goliath in terms of human enemies or besetting sins. For the interpretation in terms of physical handicaps I am indebted to a sermon on the passage by Nat H. Long.

19. 2 Sam. 11.1–12.25.

Chapter 10

1. John 3.3,7; cf. 1 John 3.9; 1 Pet. 1.3,23.

2. Matt. 22.23–33; Mark 12.18–27; Luke 20.27–40.

3. Dan. 12.2–3 is the only sure reference. See also Job 19.25; Ps. 16.10–11; 49.15; 73.26; Isa. 25.8, which have traditionally been interpreted as references to a future life, but are not generally regarded as such by modern scholars.

4. 1 Sam. 24.21; Isa. 66.22. In the Apocrypha see Ecclus. 44.14; 46.12.

5. 1 Cor. 15.12–14.

6. John 6.15.

7. Matt. 22.15–22; Mark 12.13–17; Luke 20.20–6; Matt. 5.38–48; Luke 6.27–30.

8. Matt. 26.47–56; Mark 14.43–50; Luke 22.47–53; John 18.2–11.

9. Matt. 21.12–17; Mark 11.11, 15–19; Luke 19.45–8; John 2.13–17.

10. Matt. 5.39–41; Luke 6.29.

11. Matt. 14.1–12; Mark 6.14–29.

12. Matt. 9.9–13; Mark 2.13–17; Luke 5.27–32; 15.1–2.

13. Matt. 15.19–20; Mark 7.21–3.

14. John 7.53–8.11. This story, although it is not found in some of the

earliest manuscripts of the gospel, is likely to be a faithful record of the event.

15. Luke 7.36–50. See also note 12.

16. Exod. 20.14; Deut. 22.28–9.

17. Matt. 5.31–2; 19.3–9; Mark 10.2–12; Luke 16.18.

18. Deut. 24.1–4.

19. Gittin 9.

20. Matt. 5.32; 19.9.

21. Luke 16.18; Mark 10.12; 1 Cor. 7.10–13.

22. Matt. 5.21–22.

23. Matt. 5.27–8.

24. Matt. 5.43–8; Luke 6.27–36.

25. Luke 10.29–37.

26. Matt. 15.21–8; Mark 7.24–30; Luke 9.51–6; 17.11–18.

27. Matt. 15.32–9; Mark 8.1–10; Luke 10.1–20.

28. John 4.1–30; 12.32.

29. John 10.16.

30. John 3.16–17.

31. John 8.33–59.

32. The idea of a rejected option of the gospel was previously developed in relation to the future hope in the author's article, 'A rejected option of the gospel', *Expository Times* LXXXIII (Sept. 1972), pp. 372–4.

Chapter 11

1. Matt. 16.24–6; 19.29; Mark 8.34–8; 10.29–30; Luke 9.23–5; 18.29–30.

Chapter 12

1. Matt. 13.36–43; 24.36–51; 25.31–46; Mark 8.38; 13.24–7; Luke 17.22–37.

2. Matt. 5.3–10; 6.1–18; 15.1–20; 25.31–46; Mark 7.1–23; 10.42–5; Luke 14.7–14; 18.9–14; John 13.1–20.

3. Matt. 10.5–42; 28.19–20; Mark 3.14–15; 13.9–11; Luke 9.1–2; 10.8–9; 24.45–9; Acts 1.8; John 20.21.

4. Matt. 6.19–34; 19.23–30; Mark 10.23–31; Luke 12.13–21; 16.1–13; 19–31; 18.18–30.

5. Matt. 5.33–7.

6. Matt. 5.21–2; 7.1; Luke 6.37.

7. Matt. 5.38–41; Luke 6.27–9.

8. Matt. 19.16–22; Mark 10.17–22; Luke 18.18–23.

9. Matt. 19.23–6; Mark 10.23–7; Luke 18.23–7.

10. Matt. 6.19–21,24; Luke 12.15; 16.13.

11. Matt. 5.27–8.

12. Matt. 5.31–2; 19.9; Mark 10.11–12; Luke 16.18.

13. For the rejection of the principle of retribution see Matt. 5.38–41.

14. Matt. 10.19–20; 18.20; 20.26–8; 28.20; Mark 3.13–15; 10.42–5; 13.11; Luke 9.1–2; 10.8–9; 21.14–15; 22.24–7; 24.49; Acts 1.8; John 14.16–17,26; 15.26–7; 16.13; 17.20–6; 20.21–2.

15. Matt. 26.26–9; Mark 14.22–5; Luke 22.14–23; 1 Cor. 11.23–6.

16. Matt. 28.19–20; Mark 16.16; John 4.1–3. The reference from Mark is absent from some early manuscripts and probably is not part of the original text.

17. Matt. 6.5–6; 7.7–11; Luke 11.5–13; 18.1–8.

18. 2 Cor. 12.1–4; Teresa of Avila, *Life*, E. T., J. W. Cohen (Harmondsworth 1957), pp. 187–211.

19. Luke 24.32.

Index

Abraham, 30, 57, 61, 91, 95
Acts of the Apostles, 22-8, 48, 68, 73, 74, 84, 85
Adam, 85, 87, 91, 94
Agag, 58-60, 88-9, 92
Allegory, 69, 77-8, 87-90
Allegro, John M., 132
Ambrose, 145
Amos, 82
Anderson, Charles C., 131
Apocrypha, Old Testament, 64
Apocryphal Gospels, 41-2, 140
Areas of Interpretation, 126-7
Athanasius, 63
Augustine, 60, 81, 95, 143, 145
Authentic Existence, 102
Authority, 62-6, 69-70, 128

Babylonians, 58-60, 74, 89, 95
Barnabas, Letter of, 63
Bathsheba, 57, 98-9
Bede, 60, 143
Black, Matthew, 144
Bornkamm, Günther, 132
Bowman, John W., 131
Brandon, S.G.F., 132
Brown, Raymond E., 133
Bultmann, Rudolf, 132, 138

Calvin, John, 83, 146
Carthage, Synod of, 63
Childs, Brevard S., 131
Chrysostom, John, 60-1, 143
Church
    Authority of, 62-5

Organization of, 125
Clement, First Letter of, 41
Contrast, Discovery by, 68-9, 71, 73-4, 76, 84, 92-4
Crime and Punishment, 125

Daniel, Book of, 2, 88, 89
David, 57, 61, 81, 84-5, 94, 97-9
Deborah, 94
Didache, 41
Directions in which Jesus points, 119-26
Discovery Points
    for God, 70-1, 77-9, 91-2
    for Jesus, 68-70, 77-9, 81-90
    for others, 75-9, 96-7
    for the group, 73-9, 95-7
    for the non-human creation, 77, 97
    for the self, 71-5, 77-9, 92-6
Distasteful Aspects of the Gospel, 112-15
Divorce, 25, 75-6, 108-9, 124
Docetism, 30
Dodd, C.H., 131, 133
Drews, Arthur, 132

Eisler, Robert, 132
Elijah, 61, 82, 84, 85
Eternal Life, 29, 33, 52, 104-5
Eve, 87, 91
Exclusivism of Scribes and Pharisees, 109-10, 120
Experience, Religious, 128-9
External Attitude to the Law, 109

Ezekiel, 96

Faith, as an Approach to Jesus,
    18-19
Farrar, Frederick W., 143
Father, God as, 120-1
Freedom, 103
Fulfilment of Prophecy, 81-4, 92-
    3
Future Life, 24-5, 29, 30, 33, 36,
    37, 38, 39, 41, 54-5, 105-7,
    121

Gärtner, Bertil, 140
Generality, Insignificant Level of,
    102-5
Gnosticism, 42
Guthrie, Donald, 131

Harrison, E. F., 131
Hayes, John H., 131
Hebrews, Letter to the, 38-40, 63,
    70, 85, 94
Hennecke, Edgar, 140
Hezekiah, 82
Historical Criticism, 3, 12-18
History, Bible as, 2-4
Honesty, Need for, 7-9
Hosea, 82
Hunter, A.M., 131

Identification with people in the
    Bible, 67-8
Ignatius, Letters of, 41
Illustration, in relation to
    allegory, 89
Intelligibility, Need for, 8-9
Issac, 91
Isaiah, 82-3, 88, 90, 92, 94

Jacob, 57, 84, 85, 91, 94
James, Letter of, 39, 53, 63
Jeremiah, 6, 61, 83
Jeremias, Joachim, 143

Jericho, 58-60, 78, 87
Jesus, Biblical
    as Example, 26-7, 32, 36-40
    as Saviour, 23-4, 29, 35-6, 38-
        40
    as Teacher, 24-6, 30-2, 36,
        39-40
    Acceptance of, 42-6
    Authority of, 62-6, 69-70, 128
    Identification with Rising,
        Living, and Coming
        Christ, 27, 32-3, 37-40
    Personal Characteristics of,
        24, 29-30, 36, 38-40
    Relationship to Biblical
        Christ, 18-19
    Unique Relationship to God,
        23, 28-9, 35, 38-40
    Unique Revealer of God, 23,
        29, 35, 38-40
John
    First Letter of, 39
    Gospel of, 16, 22, 28-33, 40,
        44, 52, 70, 84-6, 110, 125
    Second Letter of, 63
    Third Letter of, 63
Joseph, 88
Joshua, 58-60, 81, 87, 94
Jude, Letter of, 63
Judgement, 25-6, 32-3, 37, 39, 54-
    5, 111

Kähler, Martin, 133
Käsemann, Ernst, 137
Kümmel, Werner G., 133

Liberation, 103-4
Literary Criticism, 3, 59
Literature, Bible as, 2-4
Long, Nat H., 148
Luke, Gospel of, 22-8, 40, 78, 84
Luther, Martin, 81, 145

Manson, T.W., 131

Mark, Gospel of, 15, 21-8, 40, 84, 85, 132
Marriage, 25, 31, 36-7, 72, 108-9, 124
Matthew, Gospel of, 15, 22-8, 31, 40, 50, 70, 77, 84, 85, 124, 125
Mays, James L., 134
McArthur, Harvey K., 131
Midianite Women, 58-60, 92, 94
Montefiore, Hugh, 140
Moses, 7, 58-61, 81-2, 84-5, 87, 94-6

Nathan, 61, 82, 99
Nebuchadnezzar, 45, 102
Noah, 57, 91

Options, Acceptance of Rejected, 105-10, 120
Origen, 60, 87-9, 143, 145, 147

Parables, 2, 69, 71, 72, 77-8
Pastoral Epistles, 139
Paul, 2, 6, 7, 8, 35-8, 40, 45, 48, 50-3, 63, 69-70, 72, 74, 76-7, 85, 88, 93, 106, 129
Permissive Sex Ethic, 108-9
Perrin, Norman, 133
Person, Personhood, 102-3
Peter, Apostle, 48, 49, 72, 74, 84-5
Peter
    First Letter of, 39, 85
    Gospel of, 41
    Second Letter of, 63
Pharaoh, 57, 61, 95
Phipps, William E., 132
Prefigurement, Discovery by, 84-7, 93
Presence, Discovery by, 69, 71-2, 74, 75, 91, 93
Prophecy, 38, 50, 81-4, 92-3
Psalms, 2, 58-61, 70, 83, 89

Rahab, 58, 87
Reason, Authority of, 65
Rebirth, 104
Reimarus, Joachim, 132
Relevance of Jesus's Teaching
    Denial of, 115-18
Retribution Principle of, 59, 60, 86, 93
Revelation, Book of, 2, 6, 8, 39, 45, 48, 53-5, 63, 68, 69, 72, 77, 84, 85, 88
Robertson, John M., 132
Robinson, James M., 140
Rohde, Joachim, 134
Rollins, Wayne G., 133

Samuel, 58-60
Sarah, 94
Saul, 58
Schonfield, Hugh J., 132
Schweitzer, Albert, 131
Scripture, Bible as, 2-5
Self-fulfilment, 103
Self-realization, 103
Sermon on the Mount, 7, 14, 15, 26, 31, 48, 49, 57, 84, 109
Similarity, Discovery by, 68-9, 71-2, 74, 76, 84, 92-4
Slavery, Paul's Attitude to, 50-2
Smith, David, 131
Smith, Morton, 132
Song of Solomon, 63, 88-9
Sources of the Gospels, 15, 27-8
Spirit, Holy, 23-4, 27, 32, 37, 45, 52, 65, 70-1, 96, 119, 125, 128-30
Stephen, 26
Suffering Servant, 24, 81, 83, 93

Taylor, Vincent, 131-2
Teresa of Avila, 129, 150
Theodoret, 59-60, 143
Thomas, Coptic Gospel of, 41
Tillich, Paul, 133

Turner, H.E.W., 140
Typology, 85-7

Violence, Jesus's Attitude to, 13,
    25, 31, 36, 49, 107-8, 111,
    120, 123-5

Wealth, Jesus's Attitude to, 25,
    53, 111, 120, 123-4

Wells, G.A., 132
Wesley, Charles, 90, 143, 147
Wesley, John, 143, 147
Wink, Walter, 131
Women, Attitude of Jesus and
    Paul to, 50-1

Zechariah, 88